Micro Democracy

The democracy revolution of the information era.

By Aaron Ran

Copyright 2020 Aaron Ran

Table of Contents

Preface

While the information revolution has brought great prosperity to the economy and significantly lifted the quality of life, quietly, it is also brewing a storm in the realm of politics and social relations, destined to shake the ground of the world order. This vertigo presents a fleeting opportunity for people to build a perfect new political system to replace the broken ones, and this book offers a blueprint and action plan. However, determination and bold actions are what really matter. Most people are unprepared for sudden changes, but the presence of opportunities is precisely because, at this very moment, rulers of the old world are equally at a loss. If the fear of the unknown holds people back, the old forces will quickly regroup, cementing their advantages in technologies, turning them into a new yoke with which to dictate the masses, suffocating the hope for freedom and happiness below the shell of the old world.

To those who lived in the agricultural age, the world must have seemed endless reiterations. Then came the industrial age, and the evolution of society began to show a direction of progress, though this took a lifetime to manifest. In the information era, as the evolution of civilization has suddenly accelerated, the social transformation is unprecedented in terms of speed and scale. Staying current with new technologies has become people's essential survival skill. Microsoft took only thirty years to place "A computer on every desk and in every home,"[1] and the tide of smartphones started by Apple washed those computers away even faster: in only a dozen years, this magical little device has become a new organ attached to everyone. In a flash, we are now living in a way unimaginable to the past generation. Despite these dramatic changes, the political system is still the centuries-old design of revolutionaries on horseback. This contrast raises the question of whether the information revolution will also come to the territory of politics inevitably.

In the business world, process automation and intelligent decision-making helped to optimize production and distribution, gradually reducing the red tape, especially those inefficient and costly manual steps. Increasingly integrated supply chain systems made global collaborations more direct and efficient; new e-commerce systems shortcutted the route from the factory to the consumers. As a result, end-users influence the decisions in the production and sales procedures more directly and accurately.

In the political arena, human steps are not only inefficient but have always been prone to corruption. It is conceivable that replacing manual operations and outworn conventions with automated, intelligent democratic procedures would dramatically improve the efficiency and transparency of policymaking. More importantly, people's wills would affect political decisions more directly, so politics could better serve social justice and public interests, bringing more harmony and satisfaction to society. This vision seemed out of reach, but the developments in the economic domain have proven that once conditions are ripe, the pace of change can extend far beyond the imagination.

Before designing a new system, it is necessary to diagnose the old ones' defects, so as to prescribe the proper medicine. However, criticism is not the intent of this book. G. W. F. Hegel once proposed that *"What is reasonable is real; that which is real is reasonable,"*[2] which is often misinterpreted for justifying the unjust status quo. Despite deception and malice, this logic is not entirely unreasonable. Every long-lived political system, be it fair, advanced, perfect, or the opposite, has to be a reasonable product of the times and environments. If social material conditions and culture remain unchanged, to thoroughly transform a stable political system would be extremely difficult, if not impossible. For example, we should not lightly judge and criticize the slavery system in ancient Egypt by today's human rights and moral standards, ignoring the productivity and social reality of those times. Similarly, despite the flaws in contemporary democratic systems, we should first place them into the circumstances of their golden age, evaluate them fairly, and appreciate their superiority in their historical context. However, since the world is undergoing fundamental changes in this new era, the reform of the political system becomes the natural call of our time. It is morally righteous, feasible in implementation, and even inevitable.

Before I started writing this book, these ideas had emerged in my mind for years. This long delay was out of laziness but also humbleness. As historical trends and solutions are so evident, academics and social activists could not possibly miss them. If they were to make proposals, it would be more convincing and appealing. Regrettably, comparable theories have been shy to emerge. There once emerged some similar lines of reasoning, but people gave up easily upon encountering obvious obstacles. That being the case, I can only guess that certain experiences and qualifications have given me unique opportunities and perspectives to bring politics, business, and technology together into new conceptions. As a witness of tremendous social shifts, a world-traveling observer, and a practitioner who has contributed to current information transformations, I am convinced that the *micro-democracy* to be introduced in this book is the ultimate solution our era awaits. With the help of modern information technology, every member of an open society will be able to participate directly in the decision-making of every public affair, exercise his or her share of power in full, independently, and unconditionally. The smallest units of a democratic society, citizens, will be able to directly operate the tiniest units of democratic decision-making, issues.

Micro-democracy is hence named.

The origin of the micro-democracy theory can be traced back to the ancient "direct democracy," compared to the "indirect democracy," or the "representative democracy," which dominates today. Although the rules of direct democracy, whereby people decide on issues directly, are rather fair and straightforward, its operability declines sharply with an increase in the number of people and an expansion of territory. Thus, it has never been adopted in modern nations. While the processes of representative democracy, whereby people elect representatives to make decisions for them, are complicated with many hidden loopholes, at least it is feasible to execute in large-scale society, makes it today's dominant political structure. However, as new information and communication technologies have evolved, the problems once preventing the implementation of direct democracy have been solved one by one, and most of those solutions have been well-proven in commercial activities.

In the micro-democracy theory, direct democracy is only the foundation. Superstructures, such as human rights, social welfare, society diversity coexistence mechanisms, and civilization evolution mechanisms, are in truth its core values whose impacts are more farther-reaching. Micro-democracy is not a tinkering of isolated issues but an integrated social system and a total solution to many ills of today's political systems. Utilitarianism[3] is the final pursuit of this design; the goal is maximal overall happiness of the entire society, with fairness and openness as its guiding principles.

As the saying goes, "the devil is hidden in the details." This applies to the design and engineering of information systems, and it is no exception to the political system. By way of example, Karl Marx's communist theory once brought people a fascinating concept and grand blueprint. However, due to his early death or neglect of details of reality, too many hollows in the foundation of this splendid castle ultimately led to its final collapse. It is a common problem of many political scholars who are good at piecing together selected cases to prove their theory afterward, rather than presenting realistic foresight and guidelines beforehand. In particular, lack of specific, actionable execution plans causes the difficulty of imposing direct and substantial influences over the actual social operations. In avoiding such mistakes, this book not only discusses the concepts and principles of the new system but also pays special attention to the details at the operational level, trying to prevent micro-democracy from becoming just "another fantasy." Moreover, comprehending and accepting this theory still requires fertile imagination and an open mind. I eagerly invite readers to put aside all prejudices, explore this idea in totality, and act together for a better world in the name of people's happiness and welfare.

 # Vote

All human beings are born free and equal in dignity and rights.[1] This is the core principle of democracy. Representative democracy delivers this equality in the form of one person, one vote, which seems fair and clear, but there are fatal and elusive defects hidden behind this preconception. The two major problems are a forced transferal of civil rights and an oversimplification of equality.

In ancient Greece, all citizens could participate in open discussions of public affairs at the principal assembly, or *ecclesia*.[2] Generally, these discussions addressed specific issues: whether to build a bridge, whether to start a war, how to amend a law, and so on. Following that, the proposals ordinary citizens voted on were also about these specific matters, so the decision-making results were, without doubt, a direct and accurate reflection of the public will. Because the form of debates at the time usually favored the eloquent and passionate speakers, and because of the exclusion of slaves and women, such democratic practices were far from perfect. Regardless, this form of direct discussion and voting on specific issues was indeed a faithful interpretation of democratic principles.

However, under representative democracy, the citizens' decision-making power is forcibly transferred. On the surface, citizens all get an equal vote; however, with extremely rare exceptions (such as referendums), the issues voted on are seldom specific like building bridges, launching wars, and amending laws. Instead, the choices on the ballot become names of candidates. Furthermore, the voting focus also shifts from public affairs to the qualifications and personalities of these candidates. When citizens cast their votes, two things happen.

First, citizens give up the right to directly participate in the decision-making on actual matters. Second, citizens also transfer all their decision-making powers unconditionally to the elected candidate, regardless of whether he or she was the citizens' choice. Therefore, this ballot is not so much a proof of the citizens' democratic rights but a waiver of democratic power.

The design of representative democracy is based on a rash assumption: Under the influence of the voting power, the elected will stay loyal to their voters' wishes when making decisions, and act as spokespeople to defend their voters' interests. In reality, however, this assumption is an illusion. Ostensibly, the elected candidates gain strength from the voters, however, the privileged elites are the true masters of power. These elites control special interest groups to mislead and manipulate the electorate, and they only borrow voters' hands to pass the commissions to their servants. Therefore, the loyalty of the elected naturally goes to the privileged elites and special interest groups as they, rather than the voters, are the ones who truly arranged their successful election. It is not that ordinary people are too reckless and stupid to make good decisions, but the entire political and economic system has been built under meticulous designs of the special interest groups over the years, which gives the ruling class overwhelming advantages of control over information, public opinion, economy, and laws.

In a more mature democracy, public relations campaigns directly determine the public's acceptance of the candidates, which relies highly on sufficient financial support. Although money is not the only determinant of an election's outcome, substantial financial resources often bring candidates significant advantages.[3] In addition, plotted breaking events, control of news media, and manipulation of military/police systems to intervene with the election are also common tricks of special interest groups. These methods can often strongly affect the attitude and judgment of voters and lead to the voting results desired by the powerful.

In other authoritarian pseudo-democratic countries, election manipulation is no secret and is done systematically. By limiting the candidates' qualifications, increasing the election layers, or conducting no-margin elections, the ruling class can easily block competing candidates from critical positions, thus taking complete control over important decisions.

With this investment, special interest groups insert their agents into the policymaking circle so that they can steal public interests through these hands and enjoy plentiful returns. Meanwhile, innocent candidates become disadvantaged due to the lack of resources and their opponents' calculations. Since citizens' decision-making power is concentrated and transferred to the elected, special interest groups can indirectly and secretly dominate all state powers by buying-over only a handful of candidates during the election season. Obviously, it is much easier, cheaper, and more assured than winning the majority of the public directly at all times. It is therefore unsurprising that the representative democracy has become the handiest, most beloved tool of special interest groups. In truth, they likely treasure this system more than the average citizen. As we can see, the root cause of political corruption in today's democratic society is neither politicians' morality nor the effectiveness of the law's execution but the inherent flaw of the political system itself.

Even setting aside cases of intentional maliciousness, and focusing on the most genuine and decent candidates, another fatal defect of representative democracy is still unavoidable: The scope of decision-making is usually far beyond anybody's areas of expertise. Due to such personal limitations of the elected representatives, the decisions they make are either based on other irrelevant experiences or personal preferences, or they are influenced by the opinions of "advisers" around them. Although the opinions of these think tanks are sometimes very influential to decisions, they are usually not the choices of voters, even though their knowledge, political stance, and conflicts of interest are unfit.

To make matters worse, the term of office for elected representatives lasts for years, and early termination or replacement is nearly impossible. Over time, representatives become less sensitive to the voice of voters. During this period of power, even if individual representatives break promises to their supporters or are evidently incompetent, there is little the voters can do but wait until their terms expire. Alternatively, too short of a term can also be an issue. When an election approaches, politicians are always eager to show their achievements to please the voters and sponsors. So, they tend to focus on the short- and medium-term goals beneficial to their immediate political careers. Grand plans that require long-term vision and tenacity to implement are consciously ignored. This paradox shows that no matter how long the term, there is no perfect balance point at which society will actually benefit.

In response to the above problem, the only working solution is to abolish the representative democracy altogether. If there are no longer representatives, citizens won't have to transfer their political power to anyone and thus the focus of voting returns to the specific public affairs themselves. Also, without these middlemen, the faults in the public opinion feedback mechanism and power gridlock will cease to exist.

Oversimplifying the equality of rights is not unique to representative democracy; it is a common problem among other democratic systems as well. The main consequence of this oversimplification is that it neglects the variations among specific issues and individual citizens in decision-making, especially the difference in strength of the connection binding the two. As a result, equality in decision-making is very crude and sometimes even harmful to public interests. In microeconomics, it has been long recognized that marginal benefits are not constant and equal. This principle has been applied extensively in commercial activities and has played a vital role in the success of market economics. In today's political system, such personality differentiation has not been seriously considered. The equality of civil rights has always been simplified in the context of shared decision-making (that is, an equal decision share for everyone involved in the matter), and it usually suffers from a failure to be incorporated into a rational design, despite being the most common concept of equality. With the following examples, let's discuss the problems and how to fix them.

First, imagine a proposal for building a large dam. For residents who live close to the reservoir area, the impact can be devastating. They may have to move away from their homes that will likely be destroyed, lose farmland cultivated for generations, and abandon familiar lifestyles, livelihoods, and social relations. The residents who live farther away may enjoy the benefits of the dam, such as a more stable electricity supply and lower energy prices. For people who live in more remote areas, the impact may be minimal or none. Under such circumstances, is it fair and reasonable to give the above three types of people the same decision-making power on this proposal? Should citizens whose interests are not associated with the decision have equal say with those who have a substantial stake in it? Clearly, the answer is no. One's little joy and the enormous pain of another should not weigh equally on the scale of morality, and vice versa. The equality of democracy should not be interpreted simply as one person is equivalent to one person. It should also consider the degree of the effects on individual citizens. Abstractly speaking, it is necessary to recognize the objective difference of the connection binding the decision-making body (citizen) and the object (issue) at the micro level, quantify the intensity of such links, and then incorporate it into decision-making optimization.

To address the above considerations, micro-democracy claims that in democratic decision-making, citizens hold the extra weight of decision-making power on specific issues corresponding to the degree of interest relevance. Under this principle, when observing a particular issue in isolation, the decision-making power among people seems unequal. However, from a holistic view, equality is realized when citizens have equal access to additional decision-making power for issues that they have a more significant stake in. This rebalancing strategy contributes to the utility of society; that is, the overall happiness of its people will increase.

Some may argue that under the simple "one person, one vote" rule, the above shortcomings can be avoided if the voter considers his or her decision's impact on others. Regrettably, this puts unrealistic requirements on the ethical standards of voters. Selfishness in human motivation is a proven reality and has played a key role during the formation of modern societies and economic systems. In the case of mixed levels of social ethics, such requirements only benefit those selfish individuals. Psychological studies have revealed that the "attributive bias"[4] phenomenon results in a self-interested tendency that leads people to unintentionally underestimate the suffering of others. Therefore, even in an ideal world where people reach a noble and unselfish state, and are properly informed, it would still be impossible to improve social utility relying on this simplistic definition of equality.

Next, imagine another proposal for the nation to join an international trade treaty. The former analysis of the scheme's interest relevance suggest that such a treaty affects all citizens more or less the same, but in reality, it would more strongly impact those engaged in the international trading business. According to the interest relevance principle, the decision-making power of individual citizens should vary according to the interest bindings. However, this adjustment tends to focus on direct, short-term, and partial impacts while ignoring indirect, long-term, and global effects. As it happens, the links between the short-term impacts of international trading and industrial policies, and long-term implications are not always clear. For those without economics insights and global trading experience, some of the long-term macroscopic effects may be difficult to understand. Further, some sectors which seem irrelevant initially may have potential tight bindings with the treaty in the long run. To accurately analyze and predict overall implications, the relevant knowledge and experience of experts will contribute disproportionately.

Indeed, there has been an everlasting heated debate over populism and elitism; namely, whether the policy should be made by the emotional and short-sighted grassroots, or by the selfish and arrogant elites. Contrary to either case—both of which are flawed—micro-democracy provides a balanced, rational solution that eliminates arrogance and abuses of power. It does this by giving citizens extra decision-making power based on their education level and/or working experiences in the related domains. Unlike existing political systems, the distribution of such decision-making power only depends on the accumulated knowledge and experience of each individual citizen, not their current status or positions in institutions. As open and decentralized as this power distribution is, it will collect the total wisdom of the entire society in a balanced and fair manner. Academic authorities, government officials, and the closed elite circle will no longer hold exclusive privileges over decisions. Their minority opinions will be replaced by the knowledge of the whole public.

While every citizen may accumulate knowledge and experience in some domains, no citizen can possibly acquire knowledge and experience on everything. Therefore, there will no longer be a universal elite class. Instead, in specific domains, there will be different crowds of experts or *Domain Elites*. Since the accumulation of knowledge and experiences is a gradual, dynamic process, these so-called domain elites are only a statistical concept. There is no definite boundary or qualification to distinguish them from the public. When observing the decision-making on a particular issue in isolation, the difference in knowledge and experience will result in inequality of decision-making power among citizens. However, equality will be reflected on a higher level: Anyone can be an elite in the domains in which they have worked or studied, and no one will be an elite of all domains.

Under this design, it becomes a necessity and obligation for society to provide citizens with equal opportunities for education. Only so will they have fair chances to become elites of domains of their choice, and consequently for social equality to be achieved. This topic will be elaborated further in the chapter *Human Rights*.

For our final example, imagine a proposal for building a parking zone in a town that requires cutting down a forest to open up space. In this case, in addition to objective stakes and knowledge, there may be more factors worth considering. This forest may seem ordinary to some residents, but to other residents, it might have been a place for many of their important life events and linked with valuable memories. Since maximizing the total social well-being is an ultimate goal of micro-democracy, people's emotional appeals must be honored. That is, citizens with a stronger emotional skate in the decision should have extra decision-making power. However, emotional factors can be hard to quantify. Even within the same situation, people of different personalities may have different emotional responses of varying intensities. Fortunately, psychological studies provided some helpful insights: As people spend more time with other people, things, and places, the intensity of their emotional bond generally increases.[5] This means that emotional intensity has a direct positive relationship with timespan. With the excellent measurability, time is well suited as an indirect quantitative criterion for emotions. For the above example, the length of residency could be used as the basis for calculating people's extra decision-making power for local affairs.

Psychological and sociological studies have revealed that when people can more or less predict future affairs, their sense of security and well-being improves.[6] In addition, respect of customs and traditions usually contributes to the stability of society, which is associated with the length of time people spend with them as well.

Therefore, time, as an approximate surrogate indicator of emotional metrics and an anchor of social stability, shall be leveraged to determine citizens' extra decision-making power in local affairs. If observing decision-making on a specific local issue in isolation, a difference in the length of residency would result in inequality of decision-making power among citizens. However, again, equality is reflected at a global level: Everyone will accumulate time in their lives at an equal pace. For citizens, their time in life will always be counted in residency years somewhere and be valued equally.

To further ensure equality, a micro-democracy society should also provide citizens with freedom of migration so that they can accumulate their time of residency in the places they choose, equally and voluntarily. This will be further discussed in the chapter *Human Rights*.

From the above analysis, the micro-democracy voting right principles can be summarized as:

1. All citizens vote directly on proposals for every specific matter.
2. All citizens have equal basic decision-making power for every specific matter.
3. Citizens hold extra decision-making power corresponding to their degree of interest relevance associated with the specific matter.
4. Citizens hold extra decision-making power corresponding to their level of knowledge and experience in the domains associated with the specific matter.

5. Citizens hold extra decision-making power corresponding to their accumulated length of residency in the place with which the specific matter is associated.

6. The final decision-making power of each citizen on the proposal of a specific matter is the sum of his or her basic and various extra decision-making powers.

7. Each citizen has equal rights and opportunities to earn various extra decision-making powers.

8. The resolution is determined by the sum of the decision-making powers received by each scenario of the proposal.

To demonstrate how micro-democracy works, let's introduce a fictional nation, *Vianland*, where every citizen can access the national micro-democracy system, for voting and other operations, with personal electronic devices.

For any proposal, a voting weight is calculated for each citizen individually based on his or her personal situation. Initially, everybody unconditionally holds a basic 1.0 vote. If the proposal has apparent variations in interest relevance for different citizens, the citizens hold different extra voting weights accordingly. For example, on a decision regarding exploiting an oil field, residents within 10 miles of the drilling site hold an extra 1.0 vote, residents within 5 miles hold an extra 2.0 votes, and residents within 2 miles hold an extra 3.0 votes. If knowledge and experience would contribute to the decision's quality a significant amount, qualified citizens hold extra voting weight. In the case of the decision about exploiting the oil fields, citizens with undergraduate degrees in oil extraction, environmental protection, or energy technology hold an extra 0.5 vote; those with master's degrees hold an extra 1.0 vote, and those with doctoral degrees hold an extra 1.5 votes. Similarly, those with 5 years of related industry experience hold an extra 0.5 votes; 10 years of experience hold an extra 1.0 vote; and more than 10 years of experience receive an extra 1.5 votes. For citizens with both academic degrees and working experiences, their extra voting weights are the sum of both. If residents live near the drilling site, they also hold extra voting weight based on their length of residency to the degree of an extra 0.5 votes per year. Based on the above rules, each citizen's voting weight on the proposal is the sum of all of the above voting weights:

Final Voting weight =
basic voting weight +
interest-relevance extra voting weight +
knowledge-experience extra voting weight +
residency-length extra voting weight

Or more abstractly:

Final Voting weight =
basic weight +
interest factor weight +
knowledge factor weight +
time factor weight

The decision is determined by the sum of the final voting weights for each option, received from all voters.

It is important to note that the calculation rules and formula of the voting weights in the above examples are merely for demonstrating the principles and mechanisms of micro-democracy. They are by no means the most reasonable and appropriate configuration. This statement applies to all the examples regarding *Vianland* in this book unless otherwise stated.

In building the actual micro-democracy system, the combinations of different rules and formulas will determine the direction of the policies and will impose a dominating impact on the formation and development of society. As will be detailed in the subsequent chapters, with the self-adaptation and feedback mechanism of the micro-democracy country, these configurations will be continuously revised as time and the situation progresses; the society will enter an endless cycle of self-optimization. Such diversity and dynamics will bring extraordinary vitality to society, allowing it to grow and renew itself indefinitely. Eventually, optimal social forms will emerge out of this peaceful competition. The study of such configurations and evolution mechanisms is in itself sufficient as a branch of future political management discipline, a further discussion of which can be found in later this book.

To distinguish the self-determination from mass-determination, it is necessary to limit the scope of decision-making in which citizens can participate. All countries nowadays have implemented some regional division and hierarchy. Decomposing and distributing administrative orders level-by-level helps to carry out central policies. At the same time, this design grants certain degrees of autonomy at the regional level. Under the micro-democracy system, fairness and rationality considerations come first and efficiency of execution second when planning regional division. A detailed discussion of the formation and division of administrative areas is found in the chapter *Law*. Here it is only introduced conceptually.

The voting weight mechanism in the previous discussion is designed for improving equality in democratic decision-making. In order to make it really work, special attention must be paid that citizens only participate in the decisions of "related," rather than "any," matters. Blocking citizens from issues unrelated to them is vital for the fairness of the democratic decisions. Indeed, the root cause of "majority's tyranny against minority" is people's interference in matters that are none of their business. This situation occurs so frequently that it has become the "majority's tyranny against the majority." Everyone is likely a victim of this tyranny in some decisions, while a perpetrator in others.

In the design of micro-democracy's voting system, the interest relevance weight rules would fix the above problem to some extent. However, for decisions regarding a city's internal affairs, even if local residents hold higher stakeholder voting weights, it can hardly offset the vast low-weight votes from the total population of the entire country. Therefore, for the voting weight mechanism to function effectively, it is still necessary to isolate the decision-making scope according to its relevance to the voters. At the same time, oversimplification should be avoided so that people impacted by the policies are not left out of decision-making.

To continue with the example, suppose a city plans to excavate a large lake for environmental improvement. At first glance, this appears to be a local affair of the city; therefore, only city residents have the votes. However, if the lake construction would cause flow changes of the nearby river, affecting agricultural irrigation across downstream areas, then it becomes a regional affair of broader scope, and the downstream farming population should take part in voting. Furthermore, if the project requires national funding support, then the decision becomes a national affair, and all citizens are eligible to participate in decision-making. Whether to grant extra voting weights for past residents is also worthy of consideration.

In some circumstances, virtual circles could be used for decisions that lie beyond geographic boundaries. For example, senior citizens across the country could decide on affairs concerning the elderly, providing the rights of citizens of other age ranges are not affected. Female citizens across the country could make decisions about women's affairs if the rights and interests of different genders are not affected. Residents of the coastal region could make decisions on marine environmental protection matters, as long as the rights and interests of inland residents are not affected. In addition to the countless situations of virtual decision-making divisions, social groups and international communities could all apply these methods for democratic decision-making as well beyond the state power.

Taking into account these additional circumstances, the basic principles of micro-democracy voting can be further abstracted as:

1. People relevant to the specific matters are eligible to participate in its decisions and are referred to as the relevant voters.
2. Relevant voters hold equal basic voting weights for the decision.
3. Relevant voters hold extra voting weights based on reasonable principles and equal rules for the decision.
4. Relevant voters' final voting weight for the decision is the sum of the basic voting weight and various extra voting weights.
5. The decision is determined by the total voting weights for each option.

 # **Delegation**

Under the micro-democracy system, a practical difficulty ensues when citizens hold direct voting power over decisions on all public affairs. There are so many decisions demanding attention, timewise, energy-wise, information-wise, and knowledge-wise, all are far beyond the processing capacity of ordinary people. This could jeopardize the quality of decision-making. Clearly, organized, professional agents or institutions loyal to the public interests will be of great help for this situation. This is meant to be the role played by today's politicians and political parties; unfortunately, however, the fatally flawed representative democracy system has resulted in a total failure of adequate decision-making.

In the representative democracy, only the representatives and government officials have access to sufficient information, resources, and authority for making informed decisions. Ordinary citizens can only accept whatever decisions these representatives have made blindly and passively. As mentioned in the first chapter, when citizens vote, they automatically surrender the decision-making power on actual problems, and transfer their nominal powers to the elected. Such a power transferal essentially forms a delegation relationship between the citizens and the political agents. Regrettably, the delegation in the representative democracy is immoral for the following reasons:

Firstly, the delegation relationship in a representative democracy is compulsive. Whether or not the final elected is the candidate a citizen voted for, and whether or not the citizen is willing to delegate decision-making power to anyone in the first place, such a delegation relationship will be imposed on the people regardless. The conditions of the delegation, such as authority and terms, are all designed by previous delegates. Apart from exceptional situations, it is virtually impossible for voters to cancel or make adjustments to the delegation until the delegate's term ends. Since the rules and conditions of the delegation relationship are forced on the people, such a relationship stands on no moral grounds.

Under some autocratic regimes that fake representative democracy, the rulers can deprive dissidents' candidate qualification easily by controlling media, manipulating legal procedures, and restricting electoral conditions. Only those willing to please the ruling group are allowed into the representative body. Obviously, such a representative institution is unqualified for truly representing the people, and also incapable of responding to the public's feedback as needed for effective delegation. The upshot is a legion of puppets for which the rulers can simply pull strings. While the decision-making power is firmly held by the ruling group in a closed administrative system, the process of representative democracy is merely a ceremonial show. The real function of this ritual is to transfer citizens' nominal political power, through formal legal procedures, from the representative body to the administrative system where the ruler's will can reign free. It also provides legal protection to the government's authoritarian acts, obliterating the legality of civil resistance. Evidently, despite the carefully crafted procedure, there is no moral legitimacy to a pseudo-representative system.

Second, the delegation relationship in the representative democracy is blind. When citizens cast their votes, they do not know whether the candidate they selected will be committed to this delegation relationship in future decision-making, as there is no effective mechanism to ensure such a loyalty.

There are many restrictions on the qualifications of candidates, especially, the need for campaign funds, and the cumbersome processes block most people off. As a result, the number of candidates is out of proportion to the total population. This leaves little room for citizens to make informed decisions and forces them to blindly pick from a small gathering of imperfect choices. This blindness, in turn, remarkably magnifies the effects of promotion, packaging, and advertising, which further increases the candidates' dependency on financial supports, strengthening the sponsors' (rather than voters') influence over their decisions.

The representatives' power is too broad and blurs the voters' focus when evaluating candidates' ability to represent. Since it is impossible for candidates to have adequate domain knowledge and experience to cover all the potential decision-making areas, it is pointless to choose them based on their background and expertise in each field. Instead, voters' choosing considerations shifts to common sense, personality, identity, popularity, and often, to their appearance. In such cases, even if the elected representative is a model of virtue and genius of wisdom, their knowledge will always be insufficient. So, there is never a quality assurance of decision-making in such a system. Besides, it is highly unlikely for voters to find an ideal candidate who shares the same stances on each and every subject, making the trust questionable from the starting point. Moreover, since most future issues are unforeseeable at the time of the election, pre-testing the fitness of candidates' expertise or personal opinions is impractical.

Lies are a way of life in politics, and even more so for the representative democracy. Many promises are not fulfilled after the election. In some cases, this is due to over-optimistic and unrealistic visions, while in other cases it is simply a result of routine dishonesty. Because of the inadequacy of the feedback mechanisms, there isn't much that voters can do about it. Frustration and a sense of powerlessness can erode the trust and enthusiasm for democratic politics for many citizens. Consequently, they may adopt a cynical and spectating attitude. The vicious circle thus takes shape: Special interest groups manipulate politics and cause people's compromising and negative attitudes, and this, in turn, makes the manipulation easier and more convenient. Over time, the atmosphere of society becomes untrustworthy, passive, submissive, cynical, and self-destructive. When the public's positive attitude and participation spirit are suppressed and decay, the social order can only be maintained with force, which eventually leads to the phenomenon of a "democratic police state."

On the one hand, delegation plays a vital role in decision-making. On the other hand, fatal flaws are clearly spotted in representative democracy delegation. So, micro-democracy has to rebuild new delegation mechanisms, providing efficiency and high-quality decision-making while avoiding all the defects seen in the representative system. This new mechanism is called *Dynamic Delegation*. Here is how it works:

Citizens can choose freely from the following three methods for voting on any proposal:

The first method is *Preset Delegation*, whereby delegations are determined by the rules predefined by the citizens. These rules are combinations of proposal conditions and the delegates' selections.

The simplest delegation rule is unconditional delegation. For example, a citizen may give all his voting weights to a political leader out of deep admiration for the individual. Or, a citizen may choose to delegate all decision-making power to his or her best friend who shares the same interests and opinions.

More complicated delegation rules may introduce some conditions, such as categories of the matter's subjects or geographical regions. For example, by rules of content dimension constraints, a citizen may delegate decisions on economic issues to an economist with one rule, and on education issues to a well-known professor. Similarly, for the geographic dimension, the citizen may delegate the decision-making power on community affairs to an elder in the neighborhood with one rule, and with another rule, delegate to an administration expert in that region on proposals concerning broader areas.

The most complex delegation rules combine multiple conditions, commonly joining categorial and geographical conditions. Such condition combinations provide constraints where the rule applies, called *Decision Scope*. For example, with one rule, a citizen may delegate the decision-making powers of community security issues to a police officer in town who is familiar with the local situations, and with another rule, delegates to a senior judge in that area for deciding regional legal matters.

For an individual, the more preset delegation rules defined, the more likely decision scopes of the rules will overlap. Wherever overlap occurs, certain prioritization principles should determine which rule to apply to a specific matter. Usually, there is a natural priority ranking for the rules. Generally speaking, rules with stricter and more specific decision scopes out-prioritize those that are more generalized. For example, if a citizen defines one unconditional delegation rule and another rule specifically for economic topics, then the latter is more appropriate to apply for economic proposals. If this citizen defines a third delegation rule targeting those economic matters for a particular region, then this third rule is no doubt the most appropriate one to apply for economic proposals of that region.

Sometimes, the priority ranking among rules is not apparent. To avoid uncertainty and misunderstanding, an individual can explicitly arrange the priority ranking for rules he or she defined in the system. For example, a citizen may set separate rules for economic and legal topics. However, for a cross-domain proposal that incorporates both economic and legal factors, a predefined priority ranking can help to resolve this ambiguity.

The second method is *Temporary Delegation*, which is quite simple: For a specific proposal, an individual can explicitly assign a delegate.

The difference between the preset delegation and the temporary delegation is that the former is rule-based that can potentially be applied to different proposals over time, while the latter is applied to one specific proposal only and for one time alone. Because of this specificity, temporary delegations have a higher priority over preset delegations. For example, a citizen delegating his voting power for agricultural proposals to a well-known agronomist through a preset delegation rule. Still, for a particular seed policy proposal, he might trust a farmer friend's opinion better. Therefore, the citizen delegates the voting power for this proposal to his farmer friend through temporary delegation. In such a case, his delegation still flows to the agronomist for all other agricultural matters as per the preset rule delegation.

The third method is *Direct Vote*; that is, the citizen can cast a vote directly, by themselves. It is the simplest and most faithful realization of democratic power and is foundational to a micro-democracy. It ranks the highest in priority among all methods.

Under the micro-democracy system, citizens can adjust their delegation settings at any time, as they are no longer confined to an election schedule. Proposals of all kinds are processed continuously by the system throughout the year, each with its own voting deadline. If a citizen casts a direct vote before that deadline, then his or her voting weight for the proposal is directly counted in the final result. If the citizen does not vote before the deadline, then the micro-democracy system automatically determines his or her delegate for this proposal based on the current delegation settings, and the citizen's voting weight for this proposal flows to the delegate identified. The delegate's final voting weight is the sum of the voting weights of him/herself and those passed to him/her through delegations.

This design eliminates all the defects of the representative democracy delegation:

Firstly, the mandate of delegation in the representative democracy does not exist here. For any proposal, until the last moment of the voting deadline, citizens can always choose freely between casting the direct vote by themselves or delegating it to others. They have complete control over whether or not to delegate and how the delegates are designated. Therefore, citizens can always appoint the delegates who represent their interests and wills most faithfully at any given time. This fixes the problem in representative democracies, where citizens are forced to transfer power to the elected, regardless of their choices in the voting. It also prevents politicians from winning an election by defrauding people then abducting public opinion with a fixed term. In micro-democracy, any misconduct of the delegate may result in immediate revocations of the delegation, and those who lose credibility will lose their influences over policymaking altogether. Over time, citizens will find those real elites of honesty, professionalism, and wisdom, and grant them increasing decision-making power through delegation. This sensitive, non-stopping feedback mechanism will significantly improve the overall integrity of democratic politics.

Second, the blindness of delegations seen in representative democracies can also be avoided here. Since citizens can assign different delegates to proposals for different decision scopes, naturally, the primary concern for delegating goes to the relativity between the delegate's qualifications and the matter itself, rather than the representative's personality and identity. This will significantly improve the quality of decisions.

Under the micro-democracy system, delegates fall into the following four types:

1. *Ordinary Voter*

   The vast majority of citizens. They either cast direct votes on proposals by themselves or delegate to others. They may sometimes receive delegations from other citizens, but their primary life focus is not politics.

2. *Political Leader*

   A small number of political activists among citizens. Their civil rights are no difference from those of ordinary voters, except that their primary life focus is politics. They are more influential in social policymaking by obtaining extra voting weights from other citizens through delegations. Political leader is not a qualification or profession, but more of a role in the democratic political life. A citizen may act as an ordinary voter at certain stages of his or her life, or in specific decision scopes, while in other life stages or decision scopes, he or she may actively participate in policymaking activities, and thus be considered a political leader. Successful political leaders usually win a considerable degree of social popularity and charisma, receive broad delegations and corresponding voting weights, and engage in public affairs decision-making on a full-time basis. Of course, there is a gray zone between the roles of the typical political leader and the ordinary voter, but this distinction is not important for the follow-up discussion.

3. *Policonsultation Agency*

   Political organizations registered in the micro-democracy system. They own no voting weights by themselves, but they can accept delegations from citizens and vote on their behalf. Policonsultation agencies must declare and register the decision scopes they serve, which is called their *Policonsultation Domain*.

4. *Political Party*

A special category of the policonsultation agency. They are required to vote on all proposals in their policonsultation domains, regardless of whether delegations are in place. When a political party declares its policonsultation domain covering all the possible domains within a particular administrative region, it is called a *Regional Primary Political Party*. If such a party further declares its serving region as unlimited or global, then it is called *Global Primary Political Party* or, for short, *Primary Party*.

Political leaders, policonsultation agencies, and political parties still exist under the micro-democracy system. Policymaking is a complex project that requires well-organized research and the hard work of dedicated professionals. Institutions like policonsultation agencies and political parties are not only capable of organizing and coordinating such professional tasks but are also able to act as the spokespeople for citizens. Despite delegation to policonsultation agencies or political parties not being mandatory under the micro-democracy system, voting on all proposals is a massive workload for citizens, and finding ideal individual delegates for each decision scopes is also not easy. Considering this, for ordinary citizens, delegating voting powers to some reliable policonsultation agencies and political parties turns out to be quite a reasonable choice.

It is worth emphasizing that under the micro-democracy system, the delegation to policonsultation agencies and political parties is fundamentally different from the delegations under other political systems.

Under representative democracy, and most modern political systems, the power distribution among political parties is exclusive. To a citizen, the choice of the political party is also restricted to be one and only one. This strong exclusivity inevitably leads to intense confrontations, causing artificial divisions among people, where constant tension and conflicts become the norm of society. In the atmosphere of hostility, anxiously seeking their identity for a sense of belonging and security, people are more tightly attached to the political parties. This situation leads to political parties' absolute dominance in their relationship with citizens, making this relationship obedient-based rather than service-oriented. This twisted relationship is like an anti-democratic gene carried by the political parties, doomed to present them as collectivistic in behaviors and appearance. Without extra caution and deliberate correction, it will slowly rust the base of the open society, which will devolve into authoritarianism. To a large extent, the design of operating the democratic system with inter exclusive political parties, by itself, is the biggest hidden threat to a democratic society.

Under the micro-democracy system, citizens have complete control over delegation. They can delegate the voting powers whenever, wherever, and with whatever conditions they define, and to whomever they trust. The relationship between citizens and political parties is non-exclusive, and citizens are therefore in an empowered position. The decentralized and dynamic nature of micro-democracy delegation rules makes accumulating and solidifying power pointless. Therefore, for political parties, the goal is no longer the seizure of more exclusive power, but rather to achieve resolutions that are consistent with the vision and value of the party. Only by sticking to its ideology faithfully and serving its target citizen groups truly, can a political party maintain stable and lasting political influence. In order to realize this goal, collaborations among political parties are often wiser choices as compared with confrontation. Consequently, the tension among political parties is also eased, thereby allowing a constructive and cooperative attitude to thrive in society's atmosphere. Policonsultation agencies and political parties also play a key role in the micro-democracy decision-making procedures, which will be introduced in the chapter *Procedure*.

When everybody can delegate freely, *Delegation Relay* is inevitable. For example, Citizen A delegates his voting power for a proposal to Citizen B, and Citizen B transfers his voting powers to Citizen C. As such, a delegation relay formed. In this case, Citizen A's voting weight flows to Citizen C through Citizen B; as a result, Citizen C holds the total voting weights of all three citizens. Citizen C can then choose to cast a direct vote himself, or he can continue to pass on these voting weights to others. This relay mechanism provides ordinary citizens with flexible choices and helps to transfer more voting power to better decision-makers. However, it also introduces the complexity of processing.

One possible scenario is the *Delegation Loop*. In the above example, if Citizen C further delegates his voting power back to Citizen A, a delegation loop is formed. In such a case, everybody on the loop may mistakenly assume somebody else will cast a direct vote for them, and nobody takes action at the end, resulting in their voting weights becoming void. This is surely unintentional when they define the delegate rules. Therefore, the micro-democracy system must be able to detect the occurrence of this situation and make adjustments automatically. For example, the micro-democracy system should notify the citizen when this loop takes place. Until the citizen corrects it, the system can temporarily skip the delegation rules involved in the loop and apply the next delegation rule in the priority ranking.

Another scenario is *Void Delegation*. In the above example, if due to serious illness, death, or other reasons, Citizen C is unable to vote, Citizen B's delegation rules associated with Citizen C become void. The micro-democracy system should notify the affected citizens once it detects such a situation, temporarily skip the related rules, and apply the next applicable rule in the priority ranks until the situation is resolved, or until the citizen makes necessary corrections. When the delegation rules become permanently void, the micro-democracy system should notify the affected citizens and revoke them automatically.

The last scenario is the *Delegation Vacuum*. In the above example, if, after skipping all the void rules, there are no applicable ones left among Citizen B's preset delegation rules, then Citizens A and B's voting weights may be discarded undesirably unless Citizen B casts direct votes by the deadline. Although the simplest solution is to treat it as abstention, the high prevalence of this situation would cause the decision-making system to go into complete paralysis; thus, it is better to build a reliable safeguard strategy. The preferred solution is to request each citizen to set an additional *Protective Delegation Rule* with the lowest priority, which delegates the voting power to a primary party. Since primary parties are obligated to vote on all proposals across entire decision scopes, the delegation vacuum will be avoided. For more extreme situations, such as the dissolution of a primary party, extra measures can be introduced. For example, based on statistics of delegation data of the entire society, the micro-democracy system can maintain a dynamic ranking for all global primary political parties and can determine the default protective delegation rules for all citizens based on this ranking. As such, as long as there is one last global primary political party still functioning, the delegation vacuum can be avoided.

In addition to networks of citizens, delegation relays can also extend to policonsultation agencies and political parties. Generally, such delegation relays help improve the quality of decision-making. Policonsultation agencies not only express their own opinions but also consolidate views from other sources under certain principles and strategies. By doing so, they represent a more comprehensive and complete political position in decision-making, which attracts more citizens' delegations. However, it is reasonable to apply some constraints to prevent delegation relationships from growing too complicated and unmanageable. Therefore, any *Reverse Delegation*, such as delegations from policonsultation agencies to citizens, from political parties to citizens, or from political parties to policonsultation agencies, should be avoided altogether, as they will cause excessive complexity and confusion, and could even lead to hidden autocracy.

Since political parties must vote independently on all the proposals in their registered policonsultation domains, they don't need to delegate. The system needs political parties to function as stable and capable think tanks in policymaking, and at the same time, needs to eliminate unintentional abstention votes, i.e. the delegation vacuum. Political parties must vote no later than the voting deadline for the proposals, regardless of whether they have received any confirmed delegation. Because citizens can always change their delegation rules until the last moment, theoretically, it is still possible for the political party to receive voting delegations, making their vote effective. Even without any actual delegation, however, political parties' voting records can still help citizens to learn their political stance, expertise level, and decision-making styles.

Under the representative democracy, the representatives and government officials monopolize legislative and administrative decision-making. They are all on the government payrolls and collaborate within the same fixed inner circle. Naturally, they form an establishment class to protect their shared interests. When they are in a stronger position, this class tends to use their authority for personal gains; and, when weak, they are easily influenced and controlled by other special interest groups. Since the operation of this class tends to be rigid and close, gradually, it loses the connection with the people it was meant to represent. Separation of powers is the primary mechanism for checks and balances in many modern democracies. However, if this mechanism always operates within a closed circle among the same parasitic politicians, rotating their titles, trading their power, this instrument will result in nothing but politicians devising tricks with which to blind the public.

Like magnetic poles, the more concentrated the power and interests are, the more eagerly they pull each other together. Since increasing and expanding power are the inherent goals of political parties, their success will always draw the wealthy to form alliances or trade benefits. Weaker parties will become their puppets, and those strongest parties will simply build a political-business complex themselves. This trend will inevitably increase the gap between political parties and the masses, especially for ruling parties in power for long periods. In the end, the relationship between the two will degenerate qualitatively, and will only be able to be held together with lies and force. The longer a party is in power, the more twisted this relationship becomes, and the culture of the ruling party only becomes more corrupt and hypocritical.

Knowing that excessive concentration of power, stability, and closure of the ruling class are the origins of the problems, the micro-democracy abandons the power structure of the old systems entirely. In their place, the new delegation mechanism distributes the political power across all dimensions through the never-ending flow, so that power gathers nowhere and corruption roots nowhere.

A new reward mechanism is needed to support this new political system, so that the participants in public affair decision-making receive the necessary financial support to constantly contribute, and the entire system can operate healthily and continuously. In a micro-democratic society, researching, discussing, and voting on public affairs proposals are all considered a special kind of public service. To citizens, engaging in such work is an essential civil obligation in exchange for social welfare and security. The micro-democracy system does not mandate citizens to conduct this work themselves. If citizens are unwilling or unable to vote on their own, they can let others do it for them through delegation. However, if voting for one's own share is a civic obligation, voting for others is then an extra public service and should be rewarded.

For each vote, the delegate who eventually casts the direct vote earns the reward based on the number of delegations received. For example, for a proposal, Citizen A delegates voting weight to Citizen B, who further delegates to Citizen C. If Citizen C casts the direct vote, the final voting weights he or she puts into this proposal is the total voting weights of all three citizens. Also, he or she can receive rewards for having helped Citizens A and B to vote. To further explore this example with the political party's involvement: If Citizen C delegates to Party X instead of casting a direct vote, and Citizen D also delegates the voting weights to Party X, eventually Party X holds the total voting weights of all four citizens (Citizen A, B, C, and D), and should be rewarded after it casts the direct vote.

To avoid finances affecting citizens' choice of voting methods, this reward is paid by the government as part of the micro-democracy operation cost rather than charging citizens with a personal expense. The system needs to come up with a smart pricing model, low enough not to become an overly heavy financial burden to the government, and high enough to support full-time political work for those who receive delegations from many voters. For major parties trusted and supported by the people, rewards for fulfilling a large number of delegations will be their primary income source to cover the costs of hiring professionals. As such, a direct and healthy feedback mechanism between the citizens and the delegates will take shape, ensuring those influential delegates have sufficient resources for their political activities and to be strictly loyal to those citizens delegated to them. This mechanism will also help avoid corruption. If any problematic behavior of a delegate is exposed, it may lose a lot of delegations overnight, causing both its legal income source and political influence to vanish immediately, therefore losing its value in the eyes of special interest groups. Therefore, political leaders, policonsultation agencies, and political parties have to be more self-disciplined and sensitive, and handle conflicts of interest wisely.

As an example, *Vianland*'s price model for rewarding delegations is as follows: If the delegate casts a direct vote on a single proposal, the reward amount is 0.1% of the social average daily wage, multiplied by the number of citizens he or she serves directly or indirectly with this vote. So, if there are 1000 people delegating their voting weights to a political leader directly, or indirectly through delegation relay, then one direct vote per day can roughly support his or her full-time social work. If there are multiple proposals to vote on every day, he or she will enjoy a considerably wealthy life. If a political party were to received delegations from one million people directly or indirectly, the income from daily voting would be sufficient to maintain a professional team of hundreds of employees and cover other expenses. If there are multiple proposals to vote on per day, the income would be more than enough to support thousands of employees. As will be discussed in the subsequent chapter *Procedures*, the initiators of most proposals will be political leaders, policonsultation agencies, and political parties. To prevent them from submitting unneeded proposals for profit, and to control the government operational costs, *Vianland* also stipulates that only a delegate's top 9 most paid votes of the day are payable to them. Considering the primary purpose of this compensation is to support full-time political professionals, the vote is not rewardable if the number of delegations received for a proposal is less than 100. Based on the above rules, the compensation cost of *Vianland* decision-making operations is less than 2% of the total national personal income under extreme conditions, and the actual figure is likely below 1%. To support the nationwide political services that produce high-quality decisions, a modest 1% of personal income tax rate increase makes it an excellent bargain.

Micro-democracy pays political leaders and policonsultation agencies for their social services so that they can operate independently. However, it does not block them from receiving funds from other sponsors, as long as they make this information public. Indeed, other sources of financial support, such as personal donations, or even investments from special interest groups, eventually puts more social resources into policymaking and improves the quality of decision-making. External financial support will indeed bring tendentious or even biased opinions, but democratic politics is by design a process in which different views are exchanged, confronted, and compromised. This kind of influence is unavoidable; it will occur secretly, if not publicly. As the micro-democracy system has removed the coerciveness and lack of transparency seen in representative democracies, there is reason to believe that this financial influence has more positive than adverse effects on the outcomes of decision-making.

Citizens have control over the privacy of their political positions and voting activities. They can make the voting records and the delegation rules public or choose to keep them private. While political leaders might wisely choose to disclose more information to help them to attract more delegations, the voting records will be automatically released for policonsultation agencies and political parties in a micro-democracy system, preventing them from deceiving the public.

To summarize the basic principles of micro-democracy's voting delegation:

1. Citizens can choose to cast a direct vote independently or to delegate; the delegates may be other citizens, policonsultation agencies, or political parties.
2. Citizens' choice of independent direct voting or delegate voting shall be finalized at the deadline of each proposal by following priority ranking: independent direct voting first, temporary delegation second, and preset delegation rules last. In the case of delegation failure, the micro-democracy system shall automatically detect and skip the void rules, then apply a valid

and most suitable rule according to the priority ranking of the preset delegation rules.

3. For delegation, the voting weight is transferred from the delegating citizen to the delegate. The delegate can further delegate and pass the voting weights to downstream delegates.

4. Policonsultation agencies and political parties do not have their own voting weight, but they can receive voting weights from their delegation clients; they must declare their policonsultation domains as the decision scope of incoming delegation.

5. Citizens can choose whether to disclose their voting records and delegation rules. Policonsultation agencies and political parties must disclose their voting records and delegation rules.

6. Political parties must cast direct votes on all proposals in their policonsultation domains; the micro-democracy system uses political parties to provide default delegation rules for citizens to avoid a delegation vacuum.

7. Policonsultation agencies may choose to pass on proposals in their policonsultation domain or delegate to political parties.

8. The government provides financial rewards to delegates who cast the direct votes independently.

 # **Procedure**

Democratic decision-making is more than a simple act of casting votes but a set of well-defined operational procedures with a unique life cycle. For some smaller decision scopes, such as internal affairs of communities and social organizations, simplified decision-making procedures would be adequate. But with the growing scale of decision scopes and the decisions becoming more critical, the requirements for the procedures become more rigorous, for both national policies and government administration. The decision-making procedures of micro-democracy and representative systems are completely different in every detail, as will be presented in this chapter.

The decision-making procedure of micro-democracy it built around the objects of decision-making, i.e. decisions. In the previous discussion, we generally called such objects matters, issues, or proposals according to the context. But from the perspective of its life cycle, it can be broken down into following three primary forms:

1. *Proposal*

   The plan or suggestion formally proposed by the originator.

2. *Motion*

   After being reviewed, revised, and supplemented, a final text complying with the specifications is formed to be ready for voting; a proposal transforms into a motion.

3. *Resolution*

   The formal conclusion drawn from the voting result of a motion, as per the rules of the decision-making procedures.

The transition through the above states is driven by actions required by the democratic procedure; they fall into the following stages:

1. *Initiation*
2. *Validation*
3. *Voting*
4. *Execution*

Some terms here were borrowed from similar concepts found in the representative system. However, their meanings and applicable rules are not necessarily the same under the two different systems. Besides, in most representative polities, democratic decision-making is largely limited to the legislative area. Law enforcement and administration decisions are mostly made through executive orders by the bureaucratic system rather than democratically, even though many are legislative decisions in nature. Under the micro-democracy system, decisions of all the above categories are produced through democratic procedures. The government only makes routine microscopic executive decisions.

Detailed descriptions for each state or stage are as follows:

Initiation:

Under representative democracies, only representatives or government officials can initiate motions. Theoretically, they are supposed to act as the formal channel to convey ordinary citizens' voices and influence policies accordingly. However, there is no systematic lever to ensure they will respond to peoples' appeals or to constrain how they choose among the broad opinions wisely and find balance between the people and special interest groups. Randomness, contingency, and black-box operations are common. As the formal channels keep failing the people, again and again, in fury they turn to unconventional means which tend to be emotional, extreme, or even violent, and easily manipulated with misinformation and disinformation. Fierce mass movements are like out-of-control wildfires. Their destructive powers often exceed peoples' expectation, subsequently causing social unrest, chaos, and suffering.

Obviously, the procedural barriers set up by the representatives and government agencies must be crushed to enable ordinary citizens to initiate decision-making from the very first step. Nevertheless, this is not suggesting that anyone should be able to rashly throw any proposal into the ocean of an all-citizens debate at will. Filtering and adjustments are still necessary as this prevents many low-quality or repetitive motions from wasting citizens' energy and social resources. Also, it ensures format compliance so that citizens can accurately understand and effectively respond to the motion.

For the above reasons, micro-democracy introduces an important prerequisite for submitting new proposals—that is, to require certain public endorsements to back it up, making sure the proposal either expresses the wishes of a significant proportion of the general public or strong professional opinions. However, it is unrealistic to expect the proposal originators to collect these endorsements from a large number of citizens directly, as such a requirement would force them to spend much of their energy in seeking endorsement rather than improving the proposal's quality. Also, it would inundate every citizen with endorsement requests, to a degree beyond what anybody could handle or tolerate. Out of fatigue, people would likely ignore them altogether, even for those high quality and important ones, paralyzing the decision-making system.

Micro-democracy offers a practical solution to this problem: to infer the *Endorsement Intention* from citizens' pre-set delegation rules. When a citizen defines delegation rules in a decision scope, it's presumable that he or she agrees with the delegate's opinions and judgments in this decision scope and is happy to back the delegate to initiate proposals in this scope. Furthermore, it is also reasonable to assume that the citizen would support other citizens or policonsultation agencies his or her delegate trusts in that same scope. That is, delegation relay is also applicable for endorsement intention estimation.

Not every preset delegation rule will lead to an actual delegation relationship or to actual voting. Only after the voting deadline does the system know whether the individual had cast a direct vote independently; whether he or she had designated a temporary delegation; whether pre-set delegation rules were defined and how they were prioritized; and that it was determined accordingly, whether the citizen's vote applies to one or more delegation rules. Moreover, only at this juncture can the micro-democracy system know whether this citizen's vote fulfills other peoples' voting delegations and how much voting weight is transferred. At the time of proposal initiation, there is no way to foresee these triggering actions and future conditions, so predicting the eventual delegation is impossible. Therefore, it can only be approximately speculated that to a specific decision scope, the preset delegation rule at the top of priority ranking will most likely receive the citizen's endorsement. Based on this assumption, the system associates the endorsement intention to the delegate defined in this rule.

Because of the delegation relay mechanism, the above presumption faces a problem. To avoid the delegation vacuum, the micro-democracy system requires everybody to set protective delegation rules, appointing a primary party as the delegate for all motions. This would cause all the endorsement intentions to eventually flow to primary parties. It is surely not the accurate reflection of citizens' will, nor the purpose of the protective delegation rules. Therefore, citizens and policonsultation agencies, when in the role of delegates, need to decide whether they wish to collect the endorsement intention, or pass it on to the downstream delegates.

For a given decision scope, the total voting weight associated with the endorsement intentions received by a delegate is called his or her *Endorsement Weight*. The amount of endorsement weight reflects the delegate's mass representativeness and also indicates how influential he or she is over the proposals of the decision scopes. The micro-democracy system calculates and sorts the endorsement weight by decision scopes, where citizens or policonsultation agencies who rank high enough receive the privilege of initiating proposals in the corresponding decision scope. They are known as *Public Opinion Agents* for that decision scope.

Taking *Vianland* as an example, citizens and policonsultation agencies can define the decision scope which they are willing to serve as the public opinion agents. For decision scopes where they opted out, all their voting weights, including those received from others through delegations, are passed to the downstream prioritized delegates for calculating their endorsement weights. For decision scopes where they opted in, the applicable voting weights will not flow through but be included in their endorsement weights. Since political parties are not allowed to delegate further, they are considered to always opt in for their registered decision scopes.

Every day at midnight, the *Vianland* micro-democracy system starts to calculate the endorsement weight for each decision scope and publish the ranking of the day to the public within 2 hours. For each decision scope, citizens and policonsultation agencies ranked in the top 5% are entitled to the public opinion agent status. If there are more than 1,000 public opinion agents for a particular decision scope, only the top 1,000 can submit new proposals; the rest can only participate in the direct discussion. When the proportion of individual citizens among public opinion agents drops below 20%, extra citizens are granted such status to increase this proportion to

20%. Public opinion agents with the initiation privilege get a quota for new proposals submission based on their endorsement weight ranking.

Validation:

After submission, proposals enter the validation stage, where they go through steps such as a compliance check, content adjustment, specification alignment, and program configuration. They are then finally transferred into formal motions. These tasks are coordinated and facilitated by a neutral government institution and performed by public opinion agents. Though only public opinion agents can directly participate in these activities, the process is completely open to the public for inspection, so that other citizens can always exert immediate and precise feedback throughout the entire process. In addition to expressing opinions openly and contacting public opinion agents directly, people now have a much more powerful channel: the endorsement weight ranking. Whenever the citizens change their preset delegation rules, the endorsement weights are updated automatically, and the rankings shift. By observing the ranking dynamics, public opinion agents can refresh the public opinions daily and adjust their actions accordingly if they wish. When public opinion is strong enough, citizens can even directly remove those untrustworthy public opinion agents by sinking them in the ranking, so that the entire power landscape will change. In particular, during the validation phase of a proposal, if its original submitter loses his or her public opinion agent status, the proposal will be automatically revoked. Under the micro-democracy system, this kind of interaction happens in a regular, orderly, and peaceful manner all year round.

The compliance check is to filter out proposals not complying with the rules of democratic procedures. If the check fails, the proposal will be pending for the original submitter to revise until it meets the standards. These compliance checks include:

1. *Decision Scope Check*

   The status of public opinion agents and the privilege of submitting proposals come from the endorsement weight ranking, which is bound to specific decision scopes. When the proposal's actual decision scope does not match the original submitter's claimed or entitled scope, its content or applicable area must be corrected accordingly, or the submission will be rejected. It is important to point out that public opinion agents of a particular decision scope only have the rights bound precisely to this scope; they do not automatically obtain such status at the sub-scope level. If there is a need to address a specific matter in a certain sub decision scope, then the citizen must also qualify as a public opinion agent for that decision scope by satisfying corresponding endorsement weight ranking requirements.

2. *Jurisdiction Check*

   An unimplementable decision does nothing but waste social resources. Therefore, the proposal must conform to the realistic jurisdiction, in that the options it proposes can only target the government or citizens of the micro-democracy entity, rather than something beyond the government's control. The options should also hold a reasonable timeframe; attempts of ruling people who live in the remote future is clearly absurd. In practice, the more likely mistake is exceeding the jurisdiction authority allowed for the decision scope claimed by the proposal. For example, if a proposal declares that the decision scope is within a particular town, then its content can only address local townhood affairs, and nothing beyond that limit. Also, such a proposal can require people to behave in a certain way in this town; however, it can't conflict with national laws, such as promoting acts abusing

institutional human rights within this area, which are surely
invalid. More in-depth discussions on this topic are in chapter
Law.

3. *Duplicate Check*

   To save social resources while avoiding repeated efforts,
   duplicated proposals should be filtered out and rejected, or
   merged with recent identical or similar ones, unless relevant
   conditions have since changed dramatically, or broad consensus
   has been reached among public opinion agents.

4. *Integrity Check*

   Requirements of essential information elements vary by proposal
   types. For example, for industrial projects, in addition to the
   objectives and content, they should also include certain
   supplemental materials like the implementation plan, budget, and
   environmental impact assessments. For regulatory proposals,
   information like the impact analysis on existing regulations, law
   enforcement operational procedures, and transition plans are
   necessary. For proposals to overrule existing effective resolutions,
   documents like conflict analysis, and the termination protocols
   for the current ones should be prepared. The compliance check
   professionals will guide and assist the original submitters to meet
   these requirements and package the necessary documents for the
   follow-up discussions.

A well-prepared motion will be of good quality and have better
chances of passing. Proposals submitted by a sole initiator tend to be
self-limited and short of comprehensive. Their content and options
settings are also prone to be biased and misleading. Also, healthy
competition among different standpoints helps to improve the
proposal to achieve a win-win outcome.

The number of options for the proposals can be two ("Yes" and "No") or multiple (several alternatives plus one "None of Those"). Each option should be assigned a public opinion agent as its *Chief Spokespeople*, whose mission is to get better terms and support from the public for this option. Except for the two special options ("No" and "None of Those"), any option without chief spokesperson should be dropped. Signing up for chief spokesperson for each option is voluntarily, and higher-ranking public opinion agents have the priority for the position. The original submitter of the proposal is also entitled to be the chief spokesperson for one option of his or her choice.

The government agency arranges the communication, negotiation, and debating activities for each proposal at this stage. The chief spokespeople must attend these activities, and other public opinion agents in the corresponding decision scope can participate voluntarily. This is an important stage for opinions to be thoroughly elaborated, as various parties backing different options will compete for better terms. The original submitter will be the one holding the pen to amend the content. All these activities must be open to the public to trigger feedback mechanisms.

To prevent top-ranked public opinion agents from colluding and hijacking the proposal revision, the chief spokespeople are locked to the options they each represent, unless passively lost their status. In actual voting, the chief spokespeople must vote on the options they represent. The micro-democracy system can be configured to enforce this rule automatically.

Specification alignment and program configuration are the final steps in the validation phase. The government agency will assist the original submitter with the format and wording of the proposal to align with the standard specifications of the formal motion, ensuring that the text is clear, compliments the standards, conventions, and general public's reading habits, supplementary documents are properly attached, and states the impacts of each option comprehensively. Revision in this step is limited to wording adjustments without affecting the actual meaning of the content and options. After all the chief spokespeople had reviewed and signed off, the micro-democracy system will formally release the new motion and make it ready for voting.

After all the steps are completed, the proposal transforms into formal motion and enters the voting phase.

Voting:

The voting phase starts with the release of the motion and ends with the announcement of the voting results. In this stage, citizens are free to choose the way they would like to vote, either to cast a direct vote or to delegate. The majority of the cases would be somewhere in between: delegating the votes for most of the motions and casting direct votes on those with significant impacts to the personal interest.

Principles and rules for voting have been generally explained in the previous chapters, so they needn't be repeated here. However, beyond those that have already been introduced, there are some extra operational and procedural rules in the voting phase. The most important one is the *Two-step Voting Method*. As it is more relevant to the discussion of the execution phase, it will be detailed in the *Execution* section.

After the voting results come out, the micro-democracy system issues a statement to officially announce and confirm the final resolution. The announcement typically consists of the content of the winning option, a memorandum to record the decision-making activities, and a votes-counting statistical report.

Execution:

In micro-democracy, all legislative and most administrative decisions are within the purview of public democratic decision-making, except those microscopic operational decisions for routine, technical tasks. The government's policymaking functions gradually fade out, and it becomes the executive agency for democratic decisions.

Under representative democracy, the democratic decision-making process dies with the birth of the resolution. Whether the resolution is later interpreted and implemented correctly or not, and whether notable flaws are later found in it or not are no longer decision issues but execution issues. For amending or overturning the decision, a new decision-making process has to be started over, which is time-consuming and painful. While this is still a practical method, under the micro-democracy system, an important new mechanism is introduced which extends the decision cycle to the entire resolution execution phase. It allows the public to re-validate and change the decision and refine or terminate it if needed.

For facilitating a discussion of this new mechanism, resolutions can be categorized into four types:

1. *Irreversible Mission*
2. *Reversible Mission*
3. *Temporary Laws*
4. *Permanent Laws*

Mission type resolutions are to complete one or a series of specific tasks. They come to an end as soon as the predefined goals are achieved. They subdivide further into irreversible and reversible missions. For the former, once the execution has started, it is impossible to restore it to the original state. As for the latter, the execution can be aborted halfway, and restored to its previous state entirely or partially.

The execution time for most irreversible missions is short and can be regarded as an instantaneous action compared to the timespan of the decision-making procedure. Once started, it is either too late to suspend, or impossible to reverse the consequences. For example, cutting down a big tree or tearing down an ancient temple are representative of irreversible mission. The cut tree cannot grow back to the earlier shape, and the ancient temple in ruin will never be the original one even if rebuilt. For some other situations, the irreversible missions may go beyond people's control. Like the declaration of war, once the battles break out, the loss of life and materials will never be recoverable. Moreover, the war's progression is not a unilateral democratic decision; it will be influenced by various external factors that are not as simple as withdrawing the war resolution.

Reversible missions usually take a longer time to execute, such as cutting down an entire forest or building a large industrial park. If the resolution is overturned soon enough, there will still be chances to reverse or partially avoid its consequences. For example, once the resolution execution is terminated, although part of the forest may be unrestorable, the rest can be retained. If the project of building the industrial park is aborted, the portion already built may be unrestorable, but the unspent workforce and material resources previously planned for the rest can be spared.

There is a gray area in between the reversible and irreversible missions. The exact boundary is up to the citizens to determine through the democratic procedure. Since corrective measures for reversible resolutions can effectively curb political corruption, the more resolutions that are categorized as reversible, the further the space of political corruption is squeezed. For this reason, under the representative system, the reversibility of resolutions is deliberately ignored. The time and economic costs are often the excuses to prevent the timely re-validation and correction. Also, most decisions are made by the representatives' inner circle decision or the government's administrative orders, and then deemed "a fait accompli." The most obvious example is the presidential election: Once elected, even if his or her support rate drops instantly way below the bar, the president will still hold office for years. Similarly, for the referendum: Once the result comes out, even if public opinion quickly swings to the opposite, the decision will not be changed—at least for a fairly long time, if ever. For this reason, political forces often concoct dramas on the eve of the vote, using a script packed with public emergencies, misinformation, and mental manipulation, in order to quickly reach and lock-in decisions in their favor. By doing this, they also cleverly transfer the blame for making bad decisions to the public, using the exalted social cost of democratic decision-making as excuses to persuade people to "temporarily" tolerate the flawed decisions. Under the micro-democracy system, with the help of information technology and the redesign of the democratic procedures, the cost of the decision-making and execution adjustment is significantly reduced, and the above excuse no longer stands, making the reversible missions indeed reversible.

Law-type resolutions are used for the consistent and continuous enforcement of the designated social codes. They subdivide further into temporary and permanent laws. The only difference between the two is that the former has a preset termination time and conditions, and the latter stay active permanently until otherwise abolished by future resolutions. From the perspective of reversibility, they are both reversible, and once abolished, the potential impact in the remaining validity period is avoided. There are rare cases where some temporary laws have irreversible characteristics. Like the national emergency and martial law, there's no institutional channel to abolish them through democratic procedures. Because of the extreme nature of such enforcement methods, it often causes irreversible consequences.

Based on the above analysis, all resolutions fit into two further simplified categories: *Irreversible Resolution* and *Reversible Resolution.*

Humans are emotional. Emotions give people passion and courage to accomplish many feats, but on the other hand, fear and anger are sometimes enemies of wisdom. Numerous cases have demonstrated that when democratic voting runs into a stalemate, breaking news and extreme events often suspiciously provoke voters' irrational reactions. By riding this final tide, the manipulators behind the curtain often succeed in one fell swoop. Because impulsions also fade quickly, those plotted dramas always take place at the last minute for maximum effects. When people regain their senses, it's already too late.

Emotional choices do not always lead to bad decisions. There is no shortage of examples in history when achievements and miracles came out of passionate acts. With malicious manipulations, however, this is not the case. For reducing randomness and interferences of irrationality and reaching optimal decisions, the micro-democracy system introduces the "two-step voting method" for irreversible resolutions. The basic concept is that the first-round voting sets the initial result, and the second-round voting solidifies or corrects it; the total voting weights of two rounds for each option determines the final decision.

The *Reverse Symmetry Principle* is applied here: The leading ratio of the winning option in the first-round voting sets the reverse winning bar for the second-round voting. For example, in a two-option irreversible type motion, the winning side of the first-round voting leads by 10% more voting weights than its opponent. That is, the two options received 55% and 45% of the total voting weights. Then in the second round, the losing side of the first round must gain at least the same lead to turn around the results. For the previous example, this means that the first-round winner only needs to gain more than 45% of the voting weight (such as 60%) to win out the final resolution. Summing up the voting weights of the two rounds, the first-round winner received in total 55% + 60% = 115%, and its opponents received 45% + 40% = 85%. Therefore, the former won.

Similarly, this Two-step Voting Method applies to those motions with more than two options. The option receives highest total voting weights in two rounds wins.

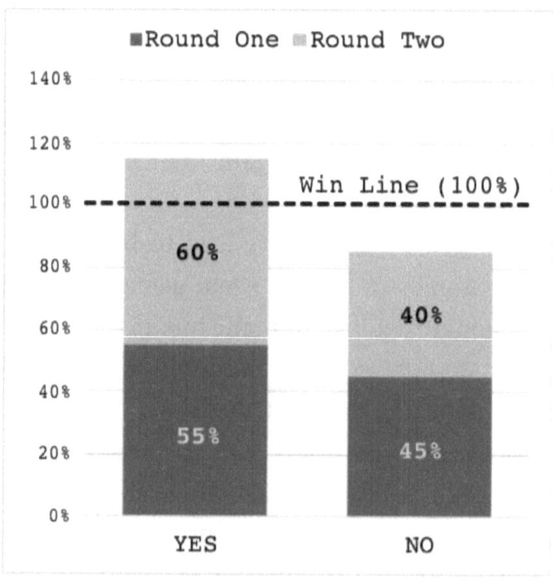

Figure 3.1: Example of Two-Step Voting Method (two options)

For such a case, even if the first-round voting result is affected by short-term disturbance, there is still a chance to correct it in the second round. The reverse symmetry principle, rather than a simple majority, used in the second round ensures such correction is a conscious and purposeful action, not another accidental random fluctuation. The first-round result should be released immediately after the voting. The cooling-off period between two rounds should be sufficient to relieve temporary anxiety, ideally more than 72 hours.

The micro-democracy system assumes people would keep their previous choices and cast the same vote in the second-round voting. Therefore, the system will repeat voters' last action in the second round automatically for their convenience, unless they cast direct votes by themselves before the deadlines. The two-step voting method mechanism works mainly where the competition runs tight. In the case of an overmatching option, one side would win a landslide victory in the first-round voting, making it nearly impossible to reverse in the second round unless unexpected happens. In this case, most people wouldn't need to do anything, as the system would automatically cast the same vote for them in the second round.

For reversible resolutions, people can also choose to adopt the two-step vote method, but it is not as necessary. This is because micro-democracy offers other opportunities to repeal them.

Various factors can affect the conclusion of the resolution, but the primary consideration is still the content of the motion. The two-step voting method solves the problem of sudden emotional disturbance. However, factors like information accuracy and external condition changes still must be taken into consideration. In many cases, only time can tell whether the decision is reasonable and wise. Also, the conclusion changes naturally as some factors may change over time. Indeed, citizens should be held accountable for their voting choices, especially those bad ones, but it does not mean decisions are carved in stone or unquestionable. Of course, active resolutions should not be overruled too lightly or too frequently, as sometimes it could cause profound waste to terminate a half-way implemented decision. For balancing these concerns, the reverse symmetry principle is also useful here for setting the pass condition for terminating active political resolutions. That is, such a new motion for overturning the original resolution needs to achieve a leading ratio no less than the winning margin the resolution previously passed with. In this way, the old decision will not be canceled too easily, and people can evaluate the resolutions' sustainability and stability by referring to the previous winning margin. For decisions that won with big advantages, people can make more and longer-term corresponding investments with confidence, and for those opposite cases, people will act with caution. As such, more social resources naturally flow in the direction where the mainstream public opinion goes.

Adjustments to the original resolution can also be made through amendments, which only change a minor portion of the original resolutions. For amendments to pass, the leading ratio must also exceed the winning margin of the original resolution previously achieved. Once passed, changes are merged into the original, and a new version of the overall resolution is formed. All subsequent execution will follow the newest version, all future amendments or vetoes will also target this version. Since each amendment introduces only minor content change, the passing threshold remains unchanged for the overall resolution so that the difficulty of amendments won't keep increasing.

The social contract[1] is the cornerstone of freedom and democracy. Although not every so-called democratic nation openly admits it, but if its legitimacy does not source back to citizens' recognition and consent of this contractual principle, then it has to seek elsewhere, such as religion or force, for the roots of its authority. Theoretically, whether a democratic country is authentic or counterfeit fundamentally depends on the degree of voluntariness and trueness of such contractual relationships. Today, ironically, citizens are rarely, if ever, given a chance to review and sign this contract. It is done for them secretly by their representatives in marble halls and behind closed doors. Even for the most critical document of all—the national constitution—very few ordinary citizens, if any, participated in or effectively influenced its drafting and voting. Of course, those initial drafters could not have obtained a legal universal mandate before any law ever existed. Given the limitations of the times and the technology of the old ages, for the time being we shall forgive this imperfection of the old systems, assuming the ordinary citizens of the time had approved the contract indirectly. After all, it is a chicken and egg paradox. However, in current times, it makes no sense and is absolutely immoral to impose this contract indiscriminately on the new generations with the same excuse.

Taking the example of the United States, the founding fathers who signed the constitution are long gone by centuries, but the generation born today is still required to inherit this contract without being asked even to sign an official consent form nor to re-discuss and re-vote. They are forced to fulfill the commitments made by others and obey the codes of conduct that they have never been consulted. It is no doubt against the spirit of voluntariness and self-determination, and consequentially invalidates the foundation of the system.

Of course, this problem is by no means unique to those mature democracies and is not limited to the constitution; actually, it's only worse elsewhere. This imposition and unfairness appear to happen to any slightly aged laws. When the older generations of citizens enacted those laws, their intention was to solve practical problems with the best knowledge and ideas at the time, not to limit future generations' right to choose. However, over time, even if the situation has long changed, some people still regard the old laws as the code of heaven, as if questioning these laws is committing a crime of treason. It is pure absurdity. This injustice presents like the elders suppressing the youngers. In truth, it is essentially a tort that the ruling class is suppressing all the people for the sake of its vested interests. Consequently, the new generation's resistance is not opposing or disrespecting the older generations but the privileged elites in the political system. Although a re-examination of archaic laws will inevitably face procedural and technical challenges, the real struggles are the obstructions by the ruling class and the special interest groups. But no matter what, these are the obstacles that micro-democracy must overcome, as this is the only righteous way for laws and nations to earn legitimacy.

Amending and abolishing resolutions are already a part of the general procedures of micro-democracy, but they require special triggering conditions such as: a sufficient leading place in the ranking of endorsement weights, proactive actions of public opinion agents, and so on. In other words, these are not automated mechanisms. For those resolutions passed with overwhelming leads, according to the reverse symmetry principle without far more than half of the total voting weights, it is impossible to amend or abolish them. Under this situation, public opinion agents would hesitate, hold back, and give up the attempts to fix the embedded problems. Imagine that some law was passed with a 90% vs. 10% advantage a hundred years ago. Since, the conditions have changed drastically, and the whole generation of citizens who voted for this law have passed away. Still, people living today can't make any change about this outdated law unless they collected 91% of the total voting weights, which is clearly against common sense, contrary to democratic ideals and social utilitarianism. Therefore, the micro-democracy system needs additional *Resolution Re-validation* mechanisms to consult new citizens automatically and timely on their opinions of the old laws still in effect, then take actions accordingly.

Operations on the information system, maintaining citizenship information, tracking citizens' dynamics and assessing the impact on the status of resolutions are all essential functions of micro-democracy. Death, relocation, or other life changes may cause citizens to flow out of decision scopes; newborn, immigrants' settlement, etc. may also add to the population for which decision scopes are applicable. When the micro-democracy system detects that the composition of citizens for a decision scope has changed significantly, it would re-evaluate the active resolutions corresponding to this scope automatically. For a particular resolution, for citizens who previously voted on the winning side and are still entitled to vote for this decision scope, if their total voting weights drop down below 50% of the current total voting weights of all eligible voters for this decision scope, re-validation is then triggered automatically.

Imagine that for a resolution, 700 citizens voted the winning option with 60% of the total voting weights. The remaining 40% of the total voting weights for the losing options came from the other 300 citizens.

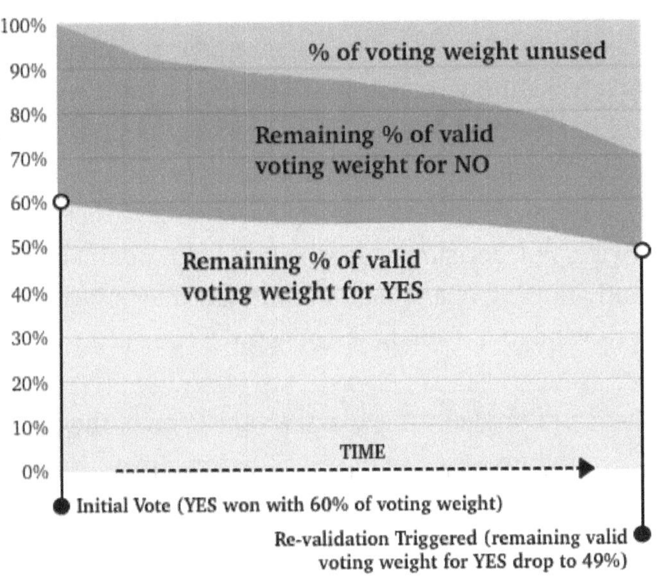

Figure 3.2: Example of re-validation trigger (two options)

Some years later, 200 citizens of the winning side and 100 citizens of the losing side flowed out of the decision scope, while 300 new citizens flowed in during the same period. Based on this latest citizen composition, if the automated re-evaluation detector found the remaining voting weights of the winning and losing sides had changed to 49% and 21%, the new citizens who had not voted hold the remaining 30%; that is, if the previous winning side now holds less than 50% of the current total voting weights, then the re-validation procedure is triggered automatically.

The main task of the re-validation is to re-vote on the current version of the resolution, to determine whether to keep or abolish it. Normally, the abolition condition no longer uses the reverse symmetry principle, but follows the simple majority principle to set the passing line. That is, 51% of the total voting weight would be sufficient to veto the original resolution. Or, if the outcome of the re-validation is in favor of the current resolution, the latest winning ratio will overwrite the previous one even if it is lower so that conditions and thresholds of future amendments are updated accordingly. When necessary, re-validation voting may also adopt the two-step voting method to filter fluctuations out of random factors. To simplify the operation, the system assumes the citizens who had previously voted on this resolution would keep their choices unless they actively re-vote otherwise. For decision scopes where large numbers of citizens are constantly flowing in and out, a minimum interval can also be set to prevent re-validation from happening too frequently.

The completion of predefined goals, the expiration of the valid period, and early termination because of re-validation, are all situations that may end the resolution execution. Adjustments of the termination conditions can only be made while the resolution is still valid. Once the resolution lifecycle ends, it is no longer resumable. If there is a compelling need to extend it afterward, it is only possible in order to initiate a new proposal, go through the standard decision-making procedure, and rebuild a similar resolution to achieve the effect of extension.

A unique characteristic of micro-democracy is that its decision-making activities do not have noticeable periodicity. All the activities are dynamically, continuously, and eternally intertwined, so that democratic decision-making can respond to the everchanging world sensitively and swiftly. This agility is a powerful feature for avoiding and correcting decision errors and countering political conspiracy and corruption. Under the micro-democracy system, the locking-in of decisions is achieved by voting weight advantages rather than fixed terms, which significantly increases the cost of political plots. Even if those dramatic performances can swindle a momentary advantage by deceiving the people, the results won't lock for long if those resolutions contradict the truth and public interests. Micro-democracy's dynamic delegation mechanism allows citizens who learn the truth to deprive dishonest politicians and political parties of power at any time, and to perform relevant corrective actions on resolutions whenever needed. It makes such speculation extremely risky, both politically and economically, and no longer profitable. This cost constraint drives political forces to cherish the public's long-term trust, while converting their attitudes and behaviors to become more honest and constructive, thereby producing a win-win outcome.

 # Human Rights

Micro-democratic decision-making can be applied to many aspects of everyday life, be it community, organization, or even corporate affairs. In these scenarios, people may choose to make compromises in fairness for the sake of efficiency and cost. However, when micro-democracy serves as the core mechanism for deciding the most serious and important issues, human rights and laws must be taken into consideration to guard the principles of fairness, rationality, and utilitarianism. Only in doing so will people enjoy all the merits and benefits micro-democracy has to offer.

The superiority of democratic morality comes down to the respect of individuals and the pursuit of total happiness of society. That is why utilitarianism serves as the core motivation of micro-democracy. Increasing the number of people enjoying civil rights and social benefits and providing these rights and benefits to the people with equality are the two main approaches to improving social utility. In micro-democracy, this is essentially a matter of human rights.

There are two prevalent views among the international community today regarding human rights:

One of the views emphasizes the equality of rights rather than their specific content. Any benefit that social wealth may provide equally is considered a right to which all citizens are entitled. From this point, as the social wealth and resource supply fluctuates (tending to grow), the standards and scope of human rights change accordingly (usually rising and expanding).

Another view of human rights pays more attention to the specific content of civil rights. Based on the functional needs of democratic systems, certain civil rights are identified as the critical conditions for the system to operate effectively. Mainly, they are those rights citizens rely on for them to independently, justly and effectively participate in political activities. In this sense, democracy and human rights share a certain degree of identity, that is, the standards and scope of human rights are tied to specific democratic systems, rather than with social wealth.

According to their different focuses, we call the former view *Welfare Human Rights* and the latter view *Institutional Human Rights*. Actually, there is no inherent difference between the two. Instead, they are complementary to each other and together complete the definition of human rights. They reveal the relationship between human rights and democracy from the perspective of cause and effect: To democracy, institutional human rights are the prerequisite; welfare human rights are the purposes. A real democratic system can only be built on institutional human rights first. Then, along with the increase of social wealth and resources, it continuously enriches welfare human rights with increased civil benefits.

Unfortunately, these two schools of human rights are easily confused, and this confusion is often weaponized in conflicts between nations. For example, some authoritarian regimes coined the concept of the so-called collective development rights, slyly painting a contradiction between civil rights and society's development. With the excuse of unique national conditions and economic development levels, they reject or forever delay the implementation of institutional human rights to preserve the ruling group's autocratic privileges. Some other developed countries have a strong sense of cultural superiority. They like to compare their welfare human rights with those of developing nations, establishing the so-called universal human rights based on their preferences. In doing so, they ignore the diversity of religion, customs, and economic conditions of societies across regions and nations. With great arrogance, they take human rights as a one-size-fits-all excuse to justify sanctions and invasions against underdeveloped countries. They selectively enforce human rights under double standards and often leave behind a much more severe humanitarian disaster after achieving their real goals, which indicates that what they cared about was not the people's wellbeing but other hidden agendas.

To solve the above problems, institutional human rights and welfare human rights are treated differently in micro-democracy, so that they can best serve the purposes they were designed for. To be specific, micro-democracy provides absolute and unconditional protection for institutional human rights, to safeguard the effectiveness of democracy's mechanisms. Also, it recognizes the relativity of welfare human rights, therefore allowing its self-determination and self-adaptation to match the social values and material levels. The constitution is the guardian of the former, and regional common laws support the latter.

Unlike many countries today, protecting institutional human rights and defining the operation protocols are the only contents of the micro-democracy constitution. Any tendentious provisions that go beyond the above scope, being it religious, political, economic, or cultural, will all be considered as additional restrictions to citizens' personal choice, and are not only unnecessary but also extremely harmful. Such controversial policies and welfare human rights can only be defined in the common laws outside the scope of the constitution. Under the micro-democracy system, common laws allow for constant adjustments of the welfare human rights and are consequently highly adaptive and responsive to the changing external conditions.

As the core of the constitution, institutional human rights are extremely crucial to the micro-democracy system. It is necessary to make a detailed analysis and precise definitions on them:

Personal Safety and Freedom

Real democracy starts with citizens expressing their true aspirations faithfully. This authenticity first relies on people's sense of safety. Under violent coercion, even if citizens have permission to participate in decision-making, their choices are only a reflection of the coercer's will. Actually, threatening using violence alone is enough to distort public opinion, not to mention the case of taking freedom and life away from people. Undoubtedly, protecting citizens' safety and freedom is a democratic system's top priority and the most critical of institutional human rights.

Direct violence against dissidents is prone to draw public attention, and in turn, opposition from the people. Therefore, many authoritarian regimes prefer to use intimidation to choke dissents in their infancy. The laws are their handiest tools for limiting citizens' choices, punishing those who dare to cross the line, and at the same time, intimidating the others, preventing them from challenging political taboos. The cleverness of this approach is that it mixes up the functional laws necessary to maintain social order with the political laws to privilege the special interest groups and ruling groups, then formalizing them through legislative procedures by the representatives' hands. Consequently, the privileged classes slyly kidnap the will of the entire country. The line between anti-privileged and anti-society is deliberately blurred, making it more convenient for the powerful to paint the rebels as criminals, then demonize, isolate, punish, or even eliminate them. In fact, some of them indeed fall into this trap, shifting from fighting the rotten system to becoming anti-society, distancing themselves from the general public. Once vested interests are incorporated into the legal system, the privileged classes can leverage this violent machine of the state, especially the police and judicial forces, to systematically and automatically persecute dissidents. Hence the anti-democratic police state is born. Its core characteristic is the presence of the political provisions in the constitution and criminal laws, such that free speech becomes a criminal act that is subject to punishment.

Therefore, an open and truthful democratic system must eliminate all politically tendentious clauses from those national functional laws that are meant to maintain the social order and democratic operation systems, especially from the constitution. It doesn't mean the political tendentiousness has no place in all the laws; instead, it is still allowed in the non-core, regional, and dynamic common laws. However, the violation punishments of this kind of law must not jeopardize any institutional human rights, especially citizens' personal safety and freedom.

Decisions on Personal Affairs

The right of deciding one's personal affairs extends the right of personal safety and freedom to the territory of social life. It further encourages citizens to form an independent and autonomous attitude and dare to express their true wishes and demands via political activities.

Personal affairs typically include marriage, occupation, religion, lifestyle, and so on. The intensity people feel about the above matters varies from person to person, so the determination of violations is not always precise at first glance. Sometimes, citizens may make conscious compromises to balance financial benefits, interpersonal relationships, and other interests, which is also the citizen's independent choice. Despite complication of the situations, there is a simple principle: Citizens' independent decisions on their personal affairs should not be interfered with in ways that threaten their institutional human rights. In other words, the institutional human rights, such as the personal safety and freedom, the right to decide on other personal affairs, as well as other rights to be covered in later this chapter, are citizens' unconditional, unnegotiable rights. There should not be a reward nor a punishment for a citizen making certain personal decisions. On the flip side, it is acceptable to influence citizens' decisions on personal affairs by trading non-institutional, welfare human rights benefits as a leverage, as these are conventional and common practices in social life.

It is worth noting that the threat to citizens' rights of deciding personal affairs come from not only governmental authorities, but also families, communities, nationalities, and religious groups, over whom another shadow casts: collectivism[1].

Under the micro-democracy political system, groups previously divided by political parties, regions, or customs will face dissociation under the "relativity" principle. Citizens need to make decisions on many proposals in their daily lives, and their decision scopes vary. So, citizens need to participate in decision-making within many different groups. In such cases, the decision-making units become more dynamic and looser, and the say of the so-called collective will be weakened in decision-making. This trend reflects the direction of social progress and the inherent contradiction between collectivism and utilitarianism in modern society. It is expected that in the new stage of democratic development, i.e., micro-democracy, individualism will gain increasing space off collectivism, and inevitably encounter fierce resistance.

Although collectivism is destined to be a major enemy of micro-democracy, it should not be denied simply by judging its values, by ignoring its positive significance in certain stages of social development.

In most times of history, collectivism has been a superior and rational form of human society. The seeds of collectivism have been long imprinted in human genes, as our primate ancestors are social animals in their own right. Being weak as individuals, in order to adequately obtain food and avoid being preyed on, they must achieve group advantage through effective cooperation and concerted action. Those simians who lived alone or failed to act quickly and effectively within a group were weeded out in evolution. The model of collective priority has survived and has been continuously strengthened in natural competition. In primitive society, absolute obedience to tribal authority is still the only chance for men to survive the wilderness. While in agricultural society, threats to individuals no longer mainly come from nature, but more and more from human society itself. The characteristics of agricultural production require people to settle in fixed locations and groups for a long time. Because of the backward technology, food production often cannot keep up with population growth, especially during natural disasters. Recurrent food shortages lead to endless conflicts and wars. In the constant fighting amidst defending and plundering food, group advantage prevails. Therefore, groups who organize actions with efficiency will easily defeat the people abandoned by groups, or groups not well coordinated. If the defeated are not slaughtered, they have to succumb to or join the winning group, eventually integrating into a more collectively organized structure and culture. So, there's no space for individualism in an agricultural society either.

With the arrival of the Industrial Revolution[2], the means of production transformed entirely. This very much resulted from the refinement of the social division of labor and the progression of intensification. Due to the massive demand for labor, the bourgeoisie released the peasants from the land and the old social relations. The politically freed and empowered workforce flowed to factories, where they lived an unfamiliar lifestyle. At this stage, discipline and teamwork became even more critical in production, and workers also obtained more strength from unions for bargaining with capitalists, indicating that collectivism was gaining ground. But at the same time, the free movement of labor also quietly led to another ideology with more profound influence: For the first time, individualism and the calling for personal freedom begin to emerge and gradually became one of the society's mainstream values. On the surface, it came out of a cultural phenomenon, but the root cause was that freedom of individuals and industrial production had reached a positive interaction.

As science and technology further progressed, the trend of robotic production refinement, automation and intelligence gradually surpassed the trend of human labor division. Accordingly, labor-intensive industries transformed into capital-intensive ones. From the perspective of the total social material supply, survival is no longer a problem for humanity. People's primary motivation for work has become the pursuit of quality of life and social status. Thanks to this material accumulation, fixed and stable social relations have changed from an absolute necessity to a personal choice. All the benefits offered by collectivism are gradually weakening and disappearing. It's foreseeable that the social value will shift to more "extreme" individualism along with the development of science and technology unless this trend is broken by major setbacks like war or natural disasters. Only with such unfortunate interruption, can collectivism restore its functional rationality and return naturally.

In summation, neither collectivism nor individualism have absolute ethical value. Instead, they arise through a process of natural selection based on the economic foundation and society's functional needs. The current level and trending of science and technology developments, as well as the generally peaceful international environments, determines that micro-democracy is bound to be pro individualistic, and only when individual freedom is achieved in the whole society, will it perform the best.

Personal affair is a rather broad concept. Some breakdown is necessary for implementing proper human rights protections. In the context of micro-democracy, they fall into the following three categories: *Core Personal Affairs* within the coverage of institutional human rights, *Non-core Personal Affairs* outside of the coverage of institutional human rights, and *Public Affairs*. The distinction between the first two outlines the definite and fixed boundaries of institutional human rights; the distinction between the latter two outlines the maximum possible boundary of the welfare human rights.

The core personal affairs that often hold a long-term, stable, and significant influence over people's well-being, such as marriage, profession, religion, and so on, are considered within the coverage of institutional human rights. Despite its significance, the scope should remain restrained, not to intrude upon the scope of the collectives. As for non-core personal affairs, it is up to the local society to determine to what extent citizens have the right to decide which are regulated by regional common laws. For example, dress code and etiquette may be attributed to civil liberties in some regions but tightly restricted in others. As culture, religion, economic conditions, and natural environment vary by region, the content and the extent of the legal protection for welfare human rights differ accordingly. These differences are spontaneous, and their objective presence is naturally accepted by the local community. It is actually the collective expression of personal freedom and individual choice, as well as cultural self-determination. When newcomers enter a community, they should respect the social values and protocols, while communities should also respect the diversity among themselves. The recognition of "inequal" autonomy rules among disparate regions is by itself a manifestation of equal right to choose.

Local common laws in a region may restrict people from deciding their non-core personal affairs, which may offend some. The micro-democracy system offers citizens three choices for dealing with such a situation: leave, endure, or change. In the first option, people may choose to move to other regions where local laws respect people's decisions over their personal affairs. As will be introduced later in this chapter, migration is another institutional human right, so citizens can relocate to any region at will. In the second option, people may choose to stay and accept the inconvenience of these regulations in exchange for other benefits offered in the region. Because common laws cannot punish people by compromising their institutional human rights, the inconvenience they cause will not be overly harsh. In the third option, people can try to change the corresponding laws per the micro-democracy decision-making procedure, as long as they collected sufficient voting weights. Given these options, citizens can decide on trade-offs based on personal circumstances and choose whichever option works best for them.

Categorizing personal affairs into core and non-core, mapping them to institutional and welfare human rights, and treating them accordingly requires reform of the present human rights system. Major human rights conventions to which the international community nowadays adheres have mostly originated from the *Universal Declaration of Human Rights*[3], which defines what decisions are considered individual freedom and subject to protection by laws. However, mandating these rules as a universal, golden standard with which all societies must comply is by itself a compulsive act. The drafters' specific cultural background inevitably limited their imagination of human rights development, often causing ridiculous contradictions. For example, Western mainstream sentiments and ideologies condemn the religious police in Muslim countries for their punishment of women not conforming to canons, deeming it as a violation of human rights. However, it considers the policemen of Western countries arresting people for public nudity a justifiable act. More ironically, at the same time, some Western countries even force their Muslim female citizens to lift their veils in public. So, who has the moral right to determine which dress on which occasion represents freedom?

For another example, the labor laws and regulations in Western countries generally stipulate the maximum working time being eight hours per day for five days. However, in many economically underdeveloped countries, due to poor tools and terrible infrastructure, the above restrictions will prevent people from producing enough products to sustain or improve their living conditions. If Westerns countries are not genuinely committed to helping these countries advance their production technology and living conditions, but only to accuse their working conditions of being inhumane, then it is either hypocrisy or cunningness. Therefore, recognizing the relativity, dynamics, and development of welfare human rights is the only honest and responsible attitude.

The differences in welfare human rights across regions and groups are the result of social diversity and furthermore dependent upon respective development stages of economics and culture. For improving the laggards, the freedom of migration and dynamic democratic decision-making mechanism plays a critical role. The former allows the regions which offered better welfare human rights to attract more population, thereby promoting the ideology, culture, and economic system behind these welfare human rights and naturally spreading them to more regions and people. Also, backflowing immigrants will bring these ideas back to underdeveloped areas, gradually change the local common laws, and improve local welfare human rights through democratic procedures. It will be a natural, constant, and peaceful process, no longer leading to misunderstandings and confrontations between segregated people. This mechanism gives life to the welfare human rights. As the society progresses, new standards and concepts of welfare human rights that conform to the spirit of the times will emerge, joining the constructive and peaceful competition of ideas, so that welfare human rights can always keep up with people's everlasting pursuit of happiness.

Personal Living Material

As long as being fed and clad are still the primary life anxieties, citizens cannot make the best decisions to achieve a higher level of happiness but instead, will settle for simple survival. According to Abraham Maslow's "Hierarchy of Needs"[4] theory, although satisfying lower level needs also produces joy, there is an inner drive for promoting this joy to a higher level. It is a need of the needs. It points to a direction with minimal internal resistance and maximal social utility gain. However, in many wealthy democracies today, under the name of "economic realities," it's still a common practice to use life essentials and social security to blackmail people and to control public opinion. It is also a common phenomenon during the formation of national economic and welfare systems to treat the wealthy with generosity and the poor with harshness. The notion of "rewarding diligence and punishing laziness" in conservative market economic theory is "rewarding the rich and punishing the poor" in reality. Micro-democracy must stop this cold-blooded manipulation, while instead bringing people a sense of security and peace of mind so that they will be confident and empowered to pursue self-actualization at a higher level. Therefore, people's access to the essential living material is considered a critical institutional human right, formally acknowledged by the constitution and fulfilled by the government.

Providing free life essentials and civil welfares for the entire population is no new concept. As many attempts in history have failed, this proposal will definitely raise doubts and objections, and these concerns deserve attention and answers.

First, institutional human rights are provided at the constitutional and global level, so they should be universal and equal. It means the living material provided by the government should be the same everywhere, whether in regions of developed economies and blessed natural conditions or in underdeveloped economies and harsh natural conditions. This principle will drag the standard to a lower end so that every region can afford to offer these resources. Although this standard will likely be too shabby for economically developed regions, the purpose of this life material supply is indeed only to provide citizens with their essential needs and the sense of security, rather than economic equality in specific social contexts. Therefore, it focuses on the fundamental and relatively fixed physical needs of people, such as essential accommodations, simple food, necessary clothing, basic medical care, and storage space for personal items.

It is necessary to point out that expecting social welfare to provide universal economic equality across a vast country is a dangerous idea. Such kind of welfare generally tends to increase unilaterally towards the upper limit social wealth can support. When the economy is flourishing, it does satisfy the citizens. However, when economic conditions deteriorate and social wealth shrinks, it becomes unsustainable. Unfortunately, people often take the benefits they once enjoyed for granted and cannot accept its downgrade with a rational mind. Moreover, this cutting down can hardly be made entirely fair in execution. Consequently, once welfare degradation occurs, severe social dissatisfaction comes along with it. This imposes an adverse impact on social stability, sometimes even resulting in catastrophic subversion and turmoil. Besides, artificial economic equality and exorbitant welfare often affect people's passion for work, and it is one of the leading causes of economic vitality decline and production efficiency inadequacy.

As the positions of institutional and welfare human rights are different, correspondingly, micro-democracy social welfare systems implement them separately. Institutional human rights only cover essential material security so that it can remain reliable and stable even during economic downturn and natural disasters. At the same time, it leaves a larger range for welfare human rights to float, allowing local societies to stimulate economics and demonstrate superiority. People in different regions can manage their specific regional welfare levels based on local economic conditions, natural environments, development philosophies, and social distribution principles. During really bad times, even without the benefits of welfare human rights, people can still live worry-free with the minimum personal material supplies provided under institutional human rights.

Of course, any universal living supply relies on a certain level of social production support, even for standards considered the bare minimum. So, is the current world production capacity adequate for meeting the needs of the population? Taking the year 2017 as an example, according to the Food and Agriculture Organization of the United Nations[5], global cereal production exceeded 2.6 billion tons, while the world population was 7.5 billion. Calculated based on the minimum consumption of grain which is 140 kilograms per person per year as set by the United Nations, only 1.05 billion tons is needed to feed the entire global population, and total food production of that year was far higher. Even if the global population reached the United Nation's estimated 11.2 billion for the year 2100, this output would still be sufficient, not to mention the technology at that time will likely increase the production further while the source and variety of food may also expand. The reality is, a large portion of grain product is currently used for feeding livestock, brewing beers, and even as industrial raw materials. In 2017, about 600 million tons of corn alone was consumed for animal husbandry, and a large amount of grain was used for manufacturing wine, condiments, and various processed foods. Still, the total grain inventory reached 700 million tons. Ironically, according to the United Nation's official report, about 9% of the world's population faced severe food insecurity in 2016, and it was only 100 million tons of food (about 4% of global output) away to completely resolve this humanitarian disaster. So, there is no material shortage preventing the micro-democracy system from providing essential food supply to the public. Indeed, there are some distribution and management issues, but these can be addressed with the right design of systems and institutions.

Sheltering is another essential element of living. Due to the complexity of the housing issue itself, the United Nations has not provided simple and clear statistics regarding its stock and supply. However, considering that there are very few humanitarian disasters caused by the lack of housing in the world today, and vacant houses are vastly abundant in many regions, there are reasons to believe that the key to fulfilling the basic housing demand is not resolving shortage, but is rather the matter of distribution.

It's worth emphasizing that the core purpose of micro-democracy providing the material supply mentioned above is not humanitarian considerations, even though that will indeed solve this problem altogether. The humanitarian viewpoint tends to swing and diverge with the critics' cultural backgrounds and subjective emotional judgments. It lacks widely accepted standards and is easily confused with value perspectives. On the contrary, the functional requirements of institutional human rights are crystal clear: Ensure the citizens participate in the democratic activities without worrying about survival or being threatened in any way so that micro-democracy mechanisms are truly functioning in actual operations.

Personal Belongings

The difference between personal belongings and the aforementioned personal living material lies in their ownership. The latter are the government's properties; citizens only temporarily use or consume them with permission. As long as the supply lasts, the government has the right to rearrange the distribution or the use of these materials, such as switching shelters for occupants, and these materials do not entitle the users to the relevant voting weights. As for the former, they are citizens' properties as protected by law. Citizens can dispose of their personal belongings at will and receive the relevant voting weights as the owner.

With the market economy dominating, personal property rights are fully protected. As the core of the market economy operation, property is power. It brings the riches substantial social influence and in turn suppresses the voice of the poor. The "invisible hand"[6] of the market economy indeed operates the economy efficiently, but it is capital rather than public interests that controls this hand. To capital, ordinary citizens' hard work and needs are trivial. In some views, this invisible hand is simply the tool for the wealthy class to command workers, except it is only more polite and restrained than the whips of the slave masters and the feudal lords. Of course, this etiquette had resulted in varying degrees of societal progress, but at the end of the day, it is still nothing more than a means of exploitation. Therefore, when people judge this economic system by its seemingly scientific and just appearance, and praise its effective operation, they should also consider its underlying drive and purpose, and whom this efficiency serves and why, while not being fooled by the little alms.

Supporters of the market economy believe the nearly divine protection of personal property is a key to capitalism's great success. This opinion makes some sense, but whether it is the only path, and whether the success of a market economy always benefits everyone in a way they like, is questionable and thought-provoking. When the power of wealth falls into few hands, the efficiency of the market actually indicates the efficiency of the public in serving the privileged, and the public's well-being is more likely to drop as this efficiency rises. For micro-democracy, how to transfer economic prosperity into social utility is a matter that deserves the most attention. Specifically, how to make the broadest percentage of the public the beneficiaries of economic prosperity, how to give people reasonable say in the distribution of material resources, and how to find balance between economic efficiency and social justice.

To resolve the above problem, micro-democracy divides the personal property into two categories: *Personal Belongings*, which are within the scope of institutional human rights, and *Personal Assets*, which are under the coverage of welfare human rights. The former refers to the personal properties for fulfilling the needs of citizens' daily lives, such as houses they usually live in, vehicles that they commonly drive, collectibles that are memorable to them, or other everyday personal items. It is protected by the constitution and brings citizens additional voting weights. The latter refers to the production materials and real estate owned by citizens for profit, as well as other personal properties not categorized as personal belongings. It is protected by regional common laws and brings no extra voting weight to the owners directly. However, through designing regional common laws, citizens can determine the form and degree of protection to apply to it, so as to fine-tune the balance point of economic efficiency and social equity. There are reasons to believe that regions that offer better protection of personal assets will attract more investments, and therefore are likely to become the final choice of the public in most areas. However, the opposite may also happen where excessive protection of assets erode the rights and interests of ordinary citizens, causing the people to eventually abandon such policies. This freedom of choice allows the people to experiment in some regions with other economic models or different lifestyles, be it spiritual pursuit, absolute equality, or other ideologies beyond our present imagination. Under this unified social framework, eventually diverse economic models, cultures, and lifestyles will be able to coexist and compete peacefully.

Migration Freedom

For micro-democracy, citizens' migration freedom has both moral and technical mandates.

Wealth of the world generally comes from two origins: robbery and creation. People did not create land, sea, space, and natural resources, so the possession of any of these can only be achieved through violent robbery and inheritance of booty. Although historical reality cannot be changed, one should not deny that this robbery is brutal and primitive. Injustice and immorality will always be attached to the booty and be passed on to the inheritors. The times we live in are in need of new ideas and rules that match the level of society's development in order for humankind to evolve from barbarity to civilization.

So how can people rightfully own the non-created wealth? On this issue, different views are held by different civilization stages and various political economy systems. Since micro-democracy has the ultimate goal of maximizing the total social utility, its first objective is to allow citizens an equal opportunity to obtain the greatest happiness from such wealth. In principle, people should have equal rights to use non-created wealth and its derivatives. The land is surely no exception as it is the most significant kind of such wealth and the focus of people's attention. The greatest joy the land can produce comes from those bound directly to it. Recognizing the privileges of actual residents and occupants, encouraging and protecting the equal rights for people to establish such direct relationships with the land, has special significance for micro-democracy. Some people may have inherited the lands by birth. However, unless spending their time accompanying the lands, they can't produce the same degree of emotional bindings with it compared to those who are true residents. The ownership of the land separated from personal life can almost always be tracked back to violent snatching and speculation. It is immoral and unequal at its root, so it is ultimately toxic to social utilitarianism and will not be recognized by micro-democracy.

For any particular land, those who live on it and accompany with it deserve the highest rights of disposal and benefits. They make decisions related to it and bear the direct consequences; hence the power and responsibility are logically bound to them. Since all people have equal rights over all lands and physical presence is the only way to acquire such rights, freedom of migration becomes a natural prerequisite for people to truly and equally exercise this right.

On the issue of migration, two prominent contradictions stand. Firstly, many of the original residents hold rejective attitudes towards new immigrants and set obstacles to block them from coming, so that the original residents can continue to monopolize local resources and enjoy current benefits. On the other hand, new immigrants usually gain the similar social welfare and political power as the original residents as soon as they settle down. When many new immigrants gather in close political groups in a short time, they can form a strong political influence, and bring radical policy changes to the region. This kind of short-term impact may very likely cause a temporary decline of social welfare and disharmony to the region. These practical problems have led many to question and oppose migration freedom, and these doubts are not unreasonable. Fortunately, micro-democracy provides the solution. With the extra voting weights based on residency history, micro-democracy gives the original residents higher decision-making power in regional affairs. They can choose to design social welfare in a way that is more beneficial to them so that they maintain a more stable lifestyle. And by separating institutional and welfare human rights, even if some welfare human rights may favor of the original residents, this won't block the free entry of new immigrants. The micro-democracy system will always protect the immigrants' institutional human rights, so that they can stand firmly on the ground, starting a new life with peace of mind. As such, the perfect balance between freedom of migration and social stability can be reached, with all people having their core concerns addressed.

Will the original residents use the voting weight advantage to hamper the migration or discriminate against new immigrants? This may indeed happen, but only to a mild extent. First of all, regional common laws have no authority to overwrite the institutional human rights protected by the constitution. Therefore, they exert no effect on for new immigrants' safety, personal living materials and belongings, freedom of migration, and other institutional human rights to be mentioned later. Although original residents can push policies in favor of their lifestyle or interests, under the constraints of institutional human rights, it is impossible for the local laws to be too harsh against immigrants. The micro-democracy system regards this mechanism as not only reasonable but also beneficial, as it takes appropriate care of the emotions accumulated by citizens over time. For new immigrants, as time goes by, they will gradually become a new generation of "original" residents of the region and will therefore gain more decision-making power with extra voting weight in the region with the fairest and most equal scale: time. Moreover, their residency history is always tracked and counted. If they decide to move back to their past residence region, they can accumulate the residence time in that region from a higher starting point and obtain the corresponding voting weights as well. From a holistic view of time and space, migrants and non-migrants are utterly equal in the way of obtaining decision-making power, except for that the former spread voting weights to more regions, whereas the latter accumulate them in a single place. Furthermore, in addition to the time-related voting weight, citizens can also earn higher voting weights from the dimensions of knowledge and relevant interests.

In the early days of micro-democracy nations, the people who have just gained freedom of migration may rush to their long-awaited dreamlands, causing a migration wave and chaos. To mitigate this impact, emerging micro-democracy governments could implement some short-term restrictions on the flow of people, but this transition should be completed as soon as possible. After the initial noise and excitement, the flow will prove moderate and orderly, and eventually becoming the normality of society.

Apart from moving freely among human settlements, people unarguably have the right to migrate to uninhabited areas. Unfortunately, most of the human-less regions on the planet are not owner-less. Through snatching, inheriting, or trading of loot, some people and groups claim ownership over those lands. However, such claims are meaningless to micro-democracy, as living on, rather than snatching, is the only legitimate way to entitle the use of the land and its natural resources. Therefore, everybody has the right to move to new territories and earn decision-making powers and interests over them. But these kinds of rights are by no means exclusive privileges, as the earth will always be the commonwealth of humanity.

Education and Work

The micro-democracy system offers citizens extra voting weight based on their education level and work experience, which improves the quality of decisions. To avoid turning these voting weights into another new privilege, the system must provide citizens with unconditionally equal education and work opportunities—in other words, giving people a fair chance to earn such power.

Most countries nowadays offer some level of compulsory education for children but leave higher education and adult education to commercial institutions. Academic and financial barriers have made education a luxury to most adults and another source of inequality. Under the current economic system, the employment rate directly affects the stability of society, sometimes even the regime. Therefore, a growing economy, which brings more jobs, has become the government's leading performance indicator. There is a general belief that increasing investment and stimulating consumption are the two most powerful instruments to achieve that. Based on this perception, the government provides business owners and capitalists with numerous favorable policies and regulations to attract investments, including monopolized public resources, tax benefits, subsidies, and so on. The true aim of these measures is to sell the public interests to help the capitalists remain on the high ground of exploitation of workers, resulting in an increasing gap between the rich and the poor, and closer alliance between the wealthy and the powerful. The economic gap will eventually transform into a political gap between the elites and the working class. On the flip side, blindly stimulating demand has led to consumerism, colossal waste, and destruction of material resources, pushing the earth's ecosystem to the edge of collapse. At the same time, the entertainment culture and commercial advertisements flood people with temptations created out of thin air, and in chasing trends exhausted people lose their ability of reflection, indulging in the endless material desires.

The advances of science and technology and the application of automation and artificial intelligence are supposed to serve society and the public. Ironically, in reality, these have become a threat to people's livelihood. As machines eat away jobs, more and more citizens have become "useless people"[7] in the market economy. Technological progress has turned into the enemy of workers. The government's typical response is to shift the employment space towards the service sector to an unsustainable extent. With the help of technology, a small percentage of the total social workforce is already enough to fulfill the material living needs for the whole population. At the same time, most laborers are in the service sector, exhausted in serving each other to meet the unnecessary made-up needs. As the skill requirements in the service sector are often lower, competition for jobs is more intense, which puts workers in a more disadvantaged position in labor relations. Modern technology already has the capability to release people from hard labor, so that they can work fewer hours, enjoy a more relaxed life; however, the reality is that the majority of workers have to work for longer hours and more years. The root of this absurdity lies in the inherent limitations of capitalism and the market economy: The profit in capitalism mainly comes from the exploitation of labor, and workers accept this exploitation because they have the needs of consumption, which is an important feature machines do not have. When capitalists cut workers, they also reduce the size and consumption capacity of their potential consumer bases and shrink their profit acquisition space. Therefore, human labor is an indispensable element for the operation of capitalism, and the increasing number of "useless people" caused by modern technology will lead to social instability and threaten the market economy itself. The ultimate result is the malfunction of the economic system, followed by the decline and collapse of the capitalist society, and the social unrest and humanitarian disasters. Therefore, providing a better economic operation model and material distribution strategy to resolve this systemic crisis, giving the doomed market economy a second life, has become a vital task for a micro-democracy system.

By redefining the right to education and including it into the institutional human rights, the micro-democracy system can fix the problems of education and economy with one solution. Not only will it save the failing market economy, but also build a safe, stable platform for the emergence, evolution, and peaceful transition of new economic operation models in the future.

Knowledge already awards extra voting weights in policymaking, for it helps improve the quality of decisions. But beyond politics, reward for knowledge is also the best investment in total societal wisdom; the return is accelerated civilization development and rapid wealth accumulation. It significantly extends the potential for improvement of life quality and happiness for the entire population, and even makes a difference in life or death of humanity. Micro-democracy's solution is to bring education into the scope of employment, turning learning into a profession, with the government paying for the efforts and results of citizens' studies. Seeing that high-quality decision-making opinions are a demand that will never be saturated, and as there will always be space and needs for technology and culture to develop further, vacancies of student positions that society can offer is unlimited. Since human, rather than material, resources are the primary supplies for the education industry, a material shortage will not block society from providing jobs in education. Involuntary unemployment will thus disappear forever.

The unlimited supply of learning jobs brings about an opportunity to resolve the economic contradictions among robotics, automated production, and manual labor. Machines will no longer be a threat to workers' livelihood but become helpers that release people from traditional industries and allow them to engage in education more conveniently and comfortably.

In principle, the micro-democracy government encourages people to expand knowledge in all directions without restriction. In practice, there may be some administrative regulations to facilitate study based on the subject's properties, as well as to design a reasonable incentive structure. Since people can always get personal living materials, the incomes from learning are not for survival but for life quality improvements. Considering that the education industry may absorb a large portion of the workforce, the student is positioned as a low-income occupation to reduce the government's financial burden and also to mitigate the impact on other industries to access labor. Actually, incomes from learning are only a minor part of the benefits for citizens; the real rewards lie in the qualifications and opportunities to access future high-income jobs, as well as the added social influence with the extra voting weights.

In the micro-democracy society, the teaching content must be unbiased and open, in order to create an equitable and safe space for different perspectives and ideas to develop freely. Although there are still distinctions between mainstream and alternative opinions, it is up to the citizens to judge and decide independently based on comparison and analysis of complete information. Mainstream or not is a statistic concept rather than official conclusions from the academic authorities. Exam scores determine not only the pay but also the voting weights, which weigh significantly on democratic politics, so examination fraud is a crime and faces severe punishment.

The channels for learning will be diverse. Apart from traditional schools, online education and virtual reality technology allow students to study whenever and wherever. Its convenience and economy make it the government's preference. Admittedly, there are still situations, such as the education of juniors, activities that require group collaboration, and subjects that require experiments and field operations, etc., where the government needs to provide necessary resources. The function of schools will change as well. Entry schools are similar to current primary and secondary schools but no longer compulsory, so that parents can make individual arrangements for the time, location, and methods of their children's education. However, as entry schools can provide safe and thoughtful care for young people and make it easy for them to earn corresponding income ("student" is the only occupation allowed for minors), this is still the wisest choice for most parents. As the government will encourage full-range, lifelong learning, and exams will have significant influences on democratic politics and social governance, the government will take over assessments and academic grading completely. Universities are no longer official educational authorities but will operate as businesses that provide efficient and comprehensive learning facilitation to adults. Other smaller commercial educational institutions will be more active and widely available. Their value will lie in providing better and specialized resources, helping people pass examinations, or teaching the knowledge and skills not yet offered by the official teaching system.

Previously, we took *Vianland* as an example to demonstrate how individuals with bachelor, master, and doctoral degrees receive corresponding extra voting weights. In reality, the universities will no longer have the function of conferring degrees; rather the government will take charge of the academic level assessments. The degree system may see major reforms in micro-democracy societies, and various rules for extra voting weights may apply accordingly.

There is a special category of education called *Basic Civic Education* that covers all the skills necessary for citizens to participate in democratic decision-making activities, generally including language, basic mathematics, logic, general knowledge of society and nature, and micro-democracy principles. Mastering these skills is a prerequisite for accurately comprehending, analyzing the content and rules in democratic decision-making, which will be the primary teaching content of entry schools. As mentioned earlier, people can also choose to learn them in alternative ways, as long as they pass the official certification exam. Once certified, citizens become entitled to participate in all political activities. Age is no longer a condition to vote. It is entirely possible for adolescents with sound comprehension to work hard and earn the right to vote way before the age of 16. For those with defective reasoning capabilities or even just lazy, older age does not automatically qualify them to vote. That being said, it is important to emphasize that this certificate is not a prerequisite for citizens to enjoy the institutional human rights and other applicable welfare human rights.

In current systems, because of the constraint of resources, most adult citizens who desire continuous learning are prevented from accessing higher education. According to statistics from the United Nations[8], even in developed countries, the per capita education period is only 12 years, which limits science, technology, and culture to advance further. The fact is, today's science and technology are already able to release a massive workforce from low-end jobs and allow them to study and better contribute to the development of civilization. The main barriers to this transformation are economic reasons: Using expensive high-tech equipment to replace cheap and repetitive labor of low-skilled workers makes no economic sense under today's market economy. Furthermore, under current social distribution rules, this will even place a direct threat to the livelihoods of undereducated workers. Therefore, the social distribution model must be changed to provide financial security for low-skilled laborers to learn and upgrade to more valuable human resources for the economy and society. And the gap of workforce caused by these transformations will make it profitable to perform and replace these no-longer-cheap repetitive works with modern technology. Thereby there forms a virtuous circle, continuously bottom-up promoting the workforce upgrade and cycling this process through the whole society. Since the working population at the bottom is usually the largest, this path of releasing human brainpower will be the most economical and efficient.

Undoubtedly, the sudden withdrawal of large amounts of labor from the bottom will hurt the economy and society. Therefore, in the early stage, the learning reward should start very low, then be gradually raised according to the actual progress, finally reaching an ideal balance between productive and learning labor. One day, social productivity will become so efficient that only a few workers will be able to produce enough materials for the entire society, and most of the population will be dedicated to study and research as a life-long career. Humans will do that which they do best, and which machines are incapable of–imagining and creating.

Right to Know

In the final analysis, decision-making is the processing of information: understanding the situation by collecting and interpreting information, analyzing it to set the expectations of results for different plans and scenarios, and finally making a choice, be it in personal affairs or national policies. Whoever controls the information supply controls the outcome of decisions. For those affected and executing, information also greatly determines their attitudes and responses, and subsequentially the final results. To politics, the advantage in information is a powerful supplement to force; its strength is often much more significant than plain violence. In an autocratic regime, the ruler's grasp of decision-making power mainly relies on force, and tightly controlling information makes the ruling much smoother and more efficient. In the age of democracy, the significance of force in governing is relatively weakened, crowning information as the true master of power. The information manipulators carefully conceal these facts in order to enjoy their privileges secretly. With their intricate news media networks, they feed misinformation to the public and put on shows of confrontations and debates among the politicians they breed, which are as fake as professional wrestling. All these entertaining tricks serve one purpose alone: create for audiences an illusion that they are the onlookers and judges of the truth, unaware of being the victims of information manipulation. For in truth that is too ugly; governments use the so-called state secrets as excuses to keep them out of the public's sight. At this point, democratic decision-making has completely deviated from its ideal and original intention and has become a trendy narcotic. As long as the manipulator instills the "right" information into the public psyche, they can get any decision they want out of democracy. The countries' so-called level of democracy is actually the scores of their information-instilling skills and theatricals. Now that information is so important, the right to know is the touchstone of the authenticity of democracy and one of the most important institutional human rights of micro-democracy. Any disguise, fraud, or concealment should be treated as an intolerably high crime in a genuinely democratic society.

Strictly speaking, there is nothing wrong with selling ideas to the public. Honest persuading and debating can help people better understand different perspectives and make sound judgments. However, intentionally covering up and spreading misinformation is a malicious act, which is a totally different case. Unfortunately, the above two types of behaviors are indistinguishable under the existing political conditions. Only with radical changes, granting citizens absolute power over information, can the public hold the truth.

Under the micro-democracy system, the government is obligated to release all the public information unconditionally, unreserved, and proactively. It is a crime for government officials to conceal, tamper with, or omit public information, whether on purpose or out of negligence. However, the authenticity requirements of information are not limited to officials, but also to ordinary citizens. If the publisher only unintentionally disseminates misinformation, he or she is obligated to correct it openly as soon as he or she becomes aware of the more accurate information. Besides, the information published in formal channels needs to be clearly classified into speculations, opinions, etc., to avoid inaccurate interpretations by the audiences.

In today's society, mainstream news organizations and information platforms are often controlled and monopolized by the ruling class and special interest groups via administrative and financial means. They use this instrument to instill an overwhelming volume of information and opinions into the public. Not only is this information often strongly biased, but also sometimes wholly deceptive. Even if the information is occasionally correct, it can still be mispresented, and end up misinterpreted. To mitigate such effects, a neutral official information index system can help the public acquire full-view information and trace its sources. Also, for decision-making activities, an official channel can give all parties a platform for public communication, especially for those who are at a disadvantage in media influence. For example, the *Vianland* government hosts an official website for supporting democratic decision-making, allows the chief spokesperson of each voting option to post a maximum of 20 minutes of video and 20 pages of text and graphics to elaborate and promote their positions.

When all the above institutional human rights function together, they will achieve the best results, maximizing social equality and utility in addition to providing high-quality decisions. However, even if only equipped with a subset of these institutional human rights, a micro-democracy country still well surpasses today's representative democracies in terms of people's happiness and welfare. According to the previous analysis, current scientific and technological capabilities and material wealth can adequately support all institutional human rights. However, situations of sudden temporary crisis that cause social materials to suffer losses or massive consumption could compromise its capacity to support the full set of institutional human rights, meaning some human rights have to be temporarily suspended or reduced. Or, for certain extreme cases like wars, it is necessary to temporarily sacrifice some institutional human rights to protect ones of greater importance.

For example, in wartime, a tremendous amount of social materials may be damaged or requisitioned for war preparation, which may affect personal living material and personal belonging rights. In addition, mobilization and deployment for the war could well restrict the rights of personal affairs decision and migration freedom. In order to succeed in military operations, it is usually necessary to take a wide range of secrecy and deception to confuse the enemy, leading to the cancellation of the public's right to know. Other examples include restricting people's movement across regions in the event of a large-scale pandemic or reducing personal material rights in the event of a severe natural disaster. It is not hard to imagine that when the crisis mentioned above occurs, the right to education is also likely to be temporarily suspended as the workforce is deployed in the battles to defend the country and human lives. As a matter of fact, in the most critical situations, not only will human rights be compromised, but the decision-making mechanism itself may need to be switched to a collective or even autocratic mode temporarily. By shelving the principle of individual priority, the nation can leverage the collective advantages to overcome immediate threats.

The micro-democracy system should prepare mechanisms to avoid creating, continuing, and expanding crises unnecessarily, protecting the economic foundation for the free society. When crises occur, it should also take extra caution for those measures that reduce institutional human rights. The goal is to prioritize restoration mechanisms, so that after the crisis relief, society will be able to return to the normal state of micro-democracy automatically, reliably, and smoothly. Such a design is one of the core contents of the micro-democracy constitution and a mandatory part of the basic civic education.

Furthermore, when arranging temporary restrictions to be imposed on institutional human rights, there is a basic principle: sacrificing those secondary institutional human rights to give priority to the more critical ones. Based on their importance, institutional human rights can be ranked as three priorities:

First priority:

- Personal safety and freedom
- Decisions power relating to personal affairs
- Right to know

Second priority:

- Personal living material
- Personal belongings

Third priority:

- Education and work
- Migration freedom

Taking *Vianland* as an example, its constitution stipulates that in the event of major social crises, temporary restrictions on micro-democracy decision-making mechanisms and institutional human rights can only be authorized by resolutions voted by the whole people. The maximal validity period of such resolutions is three months. Any extension must be approved by a vote by the entire population again, with a maximum of three months each time. Also, restrictions on institutional human rights must be as few as possible and selected in bottom-up priority order. In particular, the right to know should not be limited except for the war scenarios. Once the resolution validity period ends, the micro-democracy mechanisms and institutional human rights should be fully restored automatically, and all information ever classified as confidential during wartime must be made public.

 # Law

Laws are social conduct codes maintained by political authorities with force. They fall into three categories:

1. Oppressive behavioral requirements that reflect the ruling group's will
2. Social conventions naturally derived from the masses' shared values
3. Neutral technical protocols

Generally speaking, the latter two are complementary with people's wishes and interests. Therefore, for the most part, people are willing to acknowledge, respect, and comply. On the contrary, those oppressive behavioral requirements will inevitably be resisted by the oppressed. The higher the proportion of oppressive requirements found in the law, and the harsher they are, the fiercer the public fights back, and the more the government then depends on the law enforcement's force. In other words, the scale and strength of coercive judicial power positively relates to the proportion of oppressive clauses in laws. Based on this, people can generally inference the development level and authenticity of democracy for a given nation.

In an ideal society, legislation and public opinions are highly harmonious, and people comply with the law spontaneously. The real forces backing such laws are humanity's welfare, the sense of justice, the sense of shame, and the coercive power of the judiciary comes second. But this happens only after the first category of laws mentioned above is eliminated. This is exactly the case in micro-democracy. Since all citizens can vote directly, there is no longer a place for the ruling class in the political structure, and thus those oppressive behavioral requirements defined as the first category of laws will fade out with those elite ruling groups.

The pursuit of social utility determines the causality between mainstream public opinion and legal provisions. So, the second category of laws will constitute a majority of common laws in a micro-democracy country. As social behavior conventions tend to form spontaneously and dynamically, they follow specific life cycles. Differences of conventions in different regions, cultures, customs, and religions are inevitable. The rules of extra voting weights combined with the free flow of people result in the characteristic regional and dynamic nature of these laws. It is the exact opposite of the universality and the unity seen in modern national legal systems; it is also the main distinction between micro-democracy legal systems and those of the former.

Micro-democracy constitutions are the most obvious example of the laws of the third category. They consist of neutral technical protocols, with two main parts: The first addresses institutional human rights protection, which ensures that the decision subjects can express their will independently and authentically in democratic activities. The second part refers to democratic operation codes, which ensure the decision-making being performed is orderly and productive. Together, they build up a democratic decision-making platform that is absolutely neutral. It does not presuppose the content, nor interfere with the conclusions, maximizing citizens' self-determination. Corresponding to the two parts, the *Law of Institutional Human Rights Protection* and the *Law of Democratic Decision-making* are the two major constitutional laws of the micro-democracy system.

The third category of laws also includes other operating protocols and technical specifications that regulate daily lives, such as transportation laws, contract laws, currency laws, education laws, public security laws, and so on. They apply to all citizens nationwide and are thus called *National Common Law* or *National Law* for short.

Due to their broad influences and the need for high stability, the contents should be limited to the minimum necessary and hold a neutral position, to reduce the frequency of amendments.

Another critical design of the micro-democracy legal system is the separation of legal clause definitions and penalties. Take constitution and national laws as examples; their legal articles stipulate those mandated and prohibited acts but leave out the penalties for violations. This is because the conceptual characteristics of acts targeted by the laws are relatively clear and stable, but the punishment determination involves many more detailed considerations like complicated violation classifications, conviction criteria, and sentencing standards. Separating the relatively simple definition of act characteristics and the more tedious and inconstant punishment methods will ease the management and usage of the laws. Under this design, each law will be paired with a corresponding *Penalty Guideline* as the supplementary document which is independently revisable as per micro-democracy procedures. For example, for constitutional laws, there will be a *Penalty Guideline for Law of Institutional Human Rights Protection* and a *Penalty Guideline for Law of Democratic Decision-making* as supplementary documents. The same rule applies to other laws. For example, for the *Traffic Law*, there will be a *Penalty Guideline for Traffic Law* correspondingly.

The penalty guidelines specify the conviction criteria as well as the punishment for violations. These punishments can be defined as either specific and fixed, or as a floating range. When it is a range, further amendments can be made to it by local legislation in each sub-region, with a narrowed-down punishment range. For example, the constitutional and national laws' content and their national level penalty ranges are formulated by the entire population of the country. With the content remaining untouchable in sub-regions, people can still adjust and refine the punishments at the regional level, but the local punishment standards will never conflict with that of the national level.

For example, in *Vianland*, the *Penalty Guideline for Law of Institutional Human Rights Protection* at the national level defines the conviction criteria and punishments for the crime of theft: Stealing personal belongings worth 1,000 to 10,000 dollars is punishable by 7 to 180 days' jail time. In regions without additional amendments defined, sentencing for such crimes may land anywhere within this range. In a sub-region A, due to religious and cultural influence, local people hold a sharp resentment of such crimes. Through the micro-democracy procedure, people can release an amendment: *Penalty Guideline for Law of Institutional Human Rights Protection - Revision for Region A*. In this revision, the penalty range was redefined as from 90 to 180 days. This means that for such a crime conducted in this region, the minimum sentence is raised to 90 days in prison. Furthermore, within the territory of this region A, there's a town A1 with good economic conditions. As 10,000 dollars is a relatively small amount to the locals, people decide to revise the sentencing range to 90 days to 120 days with a new legal document: *Penalty Guideline for Law of Institutional Human Rights Protection - Revision for Town A1*. This lowers the maximum sentence for such crimes. However, the minimum penalty remains unchanged to avoid conflicts with the standard set for region A. As shown in the examples, the penalty ranges shrink as the regions narrow down, so people hold top-down control over the laws' punishment measures.

In addition to the constitution and national laws, each region can establish *Regional Common Law* or *Regional Law* for short. Regional laws fall into two categories: regional welfare human rights, and local administrative regulations.

Compared to institutional human rights, the most distinct features of welfare human rights are their relativity and fluid nature.

For example, by legislating the regional welfare human rights laws, economically developed regions can offer residents higher financial assistance standards, better working conditions, fewer working hours, more holidays, and so on. Such standards may be unaffordable to other economically underdeveloped regions. However, in situations of economic recession or natural disasters, these well-developed regions may also no longer be able to sustain the welfare human rights they once provided. In some other cases, some welfare human rights may source back to religious traditions and customs. When the social and cultural environment changes, the need for reforms of corresponding welfare human rights comes along. For the above situations, the micro-democracy decision-making process provides a solution for normalizing the dynamic adjustment of welfare human rights.

Welfare human rights provided by regional laws can be amended in any region at any level. In contrast to the penalty range's top-down narrowing-down rule, welfare human rights of lower-level regions can only improve the standards or expand the scopes of those of higher-level regions, rather than downgrading them. For example, if Region B in *Vianland* established the five-day workweek regulation, then in its subordinate town B1, residents could choose to raise the standards to four workdays weekly or expand its rules to limit daily working hours. However, this town cannot make local welfare human rights conflict with its higher-level regions, such as those demoting the standard to six working days a week.

Similar to national laws, regional laws also follow the principle of separating legal clause content and penalties. The penalties can also be revised independently as per the micro-democracy procedures, and again, the penalty range of lower-level regions must be within that of the higher levels.

Regional laws should not conflict in any way with the constitution and national laws, including how they formulate penalties. For example, criminal acts breaking the constitutional laws are either violating citizens' institutional human rights or endangering the institutions protecting them (such as the core system of micro-democracy). Following the principle of general equivalence and proportionality, the punishment should be equally aimed against criminals' institutional human rights, which usually consists of depriving them of their freedom—that is, imprisonment. However, for those acts violating only welfare human rights, the violators should not be punished by having their institutional human rights, protected by the constitution, taken away. To avoid this situation, punishments of regional laws must be limited to targeting non-institutional human rights, usually in the form of financial penalties such as fines, or deprivation of local welfare human rights.

The differences in functions of institutional human rights and welfare human rights determine the different status of the laws they correspond to. National laws play a more critical role in micro-democracy system operation, and thus must be strictly enforced by the government and the judiciary with proactive legal actions: any violation must be prosecuted unconditionally. As for regional laws, local residents can decide how these laws should be enforced: either as criminal cases initiated by the local judiciary or as civil lawsuits that go to court.

In today's civil law system[1] and marine law system[2], the principles for the determination of crimes are different. The former emphasizes the interpretation of legal texts and strives to ensure that the judgment accurately reflects the original intention of the legislators; the latter emphasizes the references of the previous precedents for supplementing and improving legal details, so that the sentencing standards among cases are fair and consistent. Generally speaking, for newly issued laws, due to lack of previous jurisprudence, the interpretation of laws plays a more important role. However, when the legal provisions are not very clear, different interpretations will lead to inconsistency or even contradictions. So, for laws enacted for a long time, referencing to precedents is generally fairer. Still, once unreasonable precedents are formed for specific situations, this unreasonableness will be inherited by subsequent cases, producing outdated and sometimes ridiculous conventions.

The micro-democracy system allows the public to create, revise, and repeal laws more actively and frequently. It makes the validity of the legal version last for a relatively shorter time, and the number of precedents will be relatively smaller. In this case, the interpretation of legal texts is usually the first choice to handle the cases. Thus, even if the text of the law is ambiguous, the cumulated precedents can still help. However, once the law is amended, the precedents accumulated against the old version should be scrapped and started over. This rule provides citizens an effective way to correct improper legal precedents. When the public finds that the precedents deviated from the original intention of the legislation, becoming absurd or no longer reflecting public opinion, people can then initiate amendments through micro-democracy procedures and issue a new version.

The stability and universality of laws help people with their long-term planning, and also to accurately predict the consequences of their own actions as well as the behaviors of others. However, the importance of such stability is overstated and often used by ruling classes and vested interests to maintain the existing order, making it extremely hard to modify and improve those unreasonable and outdated rules. This stability also creates the illusion that this artificial order is as absolute and unchallengeable as the laws of nature. Under this illusion, people are persuaded to give in to the status quo, even though it may be far from their wills or interests. On the other hand, people attempt to use the universality of the laws to put diverse social ideas and customs into the same mold, but the result is either that the dominant community forces other minorities to submit, or all communities to compromise. Although it is hard to avoid these problems altogether, an elegant hierarchical diversity design can help to reduce it substantially.

Micro-democracy legal systems trade social utility for the price of reduced stability and universality. In theory, this seems to affect people's ability to anticipate the results of behaviors and to make long-term plans. The truth is that it will shift people's attention from legal provisions back to the root of the laws: the public will. Therefore, although laws (mainly regional laws) tend to be revised more frequently, changes to the laws are not really unpredictable. As the laws reflect the values and wishes of the people more faithfully, individuals living in the society can always learn the general direction of the laws from surrounding social relationships and activities. Furthermore, when a law is passed by the vote, the voting weight advantage ratio of the winning side directly indicates the difficulty and possibility for it being overturned or revised, so that people can make fairly accurate estimations about the extent of its stability. Loopholes in the laws will be more quickly found and fixed, causing speculative conduct to decrease.

Changes of the law also concern the prosecution of past actions. As a general rule, if the lawful behavior for the old law occurred before the new ones came into effect, regardless of whether they violated the new law, they should not be punished. In some cases, during the grace period, government agencies may take preventive measures against acts that would lead to violations of the new law. However, such measures should always be limited to being preventive and non-mandatory, rather than trying to impose penalties before the new law goes into effect.

For micro-democracy, policymaking and lawmaking are no different. Citizens use the same tools and the same process for making decisions about both. The micro-democracy information system provides the same extra conveniences regarding legal assistance.

To help citizens cope with law changes, the micro-democracy information system provides many services, such as notifications, potential impact predictions, recommendations on citizen life planning, and so on. When citizens travel across regions, the system also provides regional law comparisons and reminders.

When there is no controversy on facts, the system can automate judicial decisions and enforcement. It will significantly reduce the legal costs for ordinary citizens. As the powerful no longer hold overwhelming legal resources, social injustice is more likely reduced and prevented. However, it is worth emphasizing that the automation of judicial processing is only an auxiliary tool and is by no means a replacement for human rulings. In terms of legal decisions, humans always hold the highest authority; the system's automated judgments will never be the final ruling under any circumstances. The micro-democracy information system is also the channel for legal appeals and rights protection for citizens. As long as any party raises objections and appeals through this channel, the automatically processed case must be re-ruled through human judicial procedures.

Legal provisions are formulated mainly for general situations and can be quite abstract and generic. Usually, they meet people's expectations of convictions and sentencing for common violations. Inevitably, there will always be exceptions where the convictions and punishments set by law significantly deviate from public perception and affection. Regarding these kinds of "reasonable but unlawful" cases, there are two typical views. Many believe this is a price a society of laws has to pay. Only by adhering to the absolute authority of the law and eliminating the so-called exceptional cases can the disruption of the seriousness of the rules be prevented, and can corruption be avoided. But many others argue that laws are fundamentally the reflection of people's values and wishes. When the original intention of legislation is not accurately represented due to flaws in the structure or wordings of the legal text, the actual intention of the law should be clarified and rule through making corrections by exceptional operations. As both above viewpoints have their rationales and drawbacks, in the micro-democracy legal system, the paradox is gracefully circumvented by democratic means. First of all, cases with clear facts and simple logic will adopt advanced automation and intelligence for processing. The remaining instances requiring human ruling should be transparent to the public as much as possible. For cases already convicted, pardons or commutations are allowed in exceptional circumstances. But this is no longer up to the government officials, but people's decisions on the appeal proposals made through the democratic procedure. Obviously, to limit interference with daily judicial activities, the criteria for such appeals should be very rigorous. For example, in *Vianland*, citizens can appeal to change the decision for a sentenced case, as a special type of proposal, for which the acceptance line is 70% of the endorsement weight, and the passing line is 90% of the total voting weights.

Ideally, the jurisdiction of laws should strictly correspond to the division of administrative regions, so that policies and laws across regions are concordant and fair. In particular, for micro-democracy, there's no fundamental difference between administrative and legislative decision-making, so this unity is rational and also inevitable. At the same time, the administrative region should be a reflection of the actual social composition—that is, to reflect certain shared public opinions, which usually correspond to the mainstream social group in the region. Because the composition of regional social groups is dynamic in itself, adjacent administrative regions should also adapt to keep with it, whether through boundary adjustments, merging, or further division. Furthermore, the mainstream social groups at this level may subdivide into branch social groups. It may also be reasonable to introduce sub-administrative regions within these regions.

For practical reasons, such adjustments should not occur so frequently as to exhaust the administrative and judicial institutions or disturbing societal operations. Taking *Vianland* as an example, such modifications need to meet the following conditions to become a valid proposal:

To divide an administrative region or to add a lower-level one, these conditions should all be met:

1. In any circular area with a radius of 50 kilometers or more, or any other continuous-shaped area with an area of 2,000 square kilometers or more, the population composition has changed by more than 30% (move in, move out, or natural change).
2. The immediate higher-level administrative region has not been re-divided within the last five years.
3. More than 50% of the population in the region has explicitly requested the re-division.

To merge administrative regions, these conditions should all be met:

1. All administrative regions involved have not been re-divided within the past two years.
2. More than 30% of the population in each involved administrative region has explicitly requested the re-division.

Adjusting the boundaries of adjacent administrative regions should be done in two steps: splitting, then recombining. A new administrative region should first inherit the entire set of laws from an existing region to avoid a legal vacuum and then gradually improve and refine through democratic procedures.

With the overlap of administrative regions and legal jurisdictions, whether their staff should operate more closely, integrated and merged, or more independently, is a vital decision. In many of today's governments, regardless of whether the above two frameworks are independent in terms of institutional setting or only in name, their staff have established a stable and close cooperative relationship in operation. This kind of long-term and stable collaborative relationship improves the efficiency of law enforcement on one hand. Still, it is also common that such an alliance affects the fairness of justice. Especially in some legal disputes where one side is comprised of citizens, and the other administrative agencies or officials, the judicial institutions often tend to favor the latter because of their connections and collaborations, as the temptation of power trading is usually hard to resist.

For the sake of judicial standardization and to avoid corruption, it is wiser to operate the legal system independently from the administrative system, which means that a unified judiciary needs to be built across the country's entire territory to manage and deploy the *Legal Grid* consistently. This system will service national and regional legal tasks at the same time. When the laws or the administrative regions change, the judiciary usually does not need to alter the internal organization and staffing for it, but only needs to update the settings of the applicable laws of the affected legal grid cells and follow the new settings in subsequent judicial activities. Although dynamically deployed personnel are sometimes necessary to handle the workload of legal tasks, even in this case, the regional jurisdiction and hierarchy of the grid can remain stable. It is conceivable that for specific law enforcement officers, it is possible that in the area under their jurisdiction, or legal grid cells, they will need to enforce different then-latest laws at different times. This kind of law enforcement adjustment will become a regular practice in micro-democracy and adapting such changes will become a basic skill for judicial institutions and personnel. This situation also puts automation into a more active role, helping improve fairness and impartiality by reducing human fallacies in legal activities.

 # Government

In micro-democracy, citizens take back the decision-making power from the hands of the government. Representative agents, heads of state, members of parliament, and governmental decision-making bodies all lose their positions in the political system. The new political leaders, policonsultation agencies, and political parties may still be around, but their roles are transformed into secondary and truly public services. Due to its open and dynamic nature, they are no longer a part of the government and will finally give back the center of the stage to the people. As for the government, it is no longer the policymaker, but the executor and maintainer of public policies. However, it still has some important functions to serve:

First of all, there should be a *System Department*. Its mission will be to ensure reliable operation of micro-democracy information systems, which includes building, running, and maintaining the information systems, securing the regular services of the infrastructure, managing and distributing the personal devices, and assisting the citizens to use the equipment effectively to operate on the micro-democracy system.

Second, the *Execution Department* is responsible for managing and coordinating the implementation and execution of the resolutions. Once the resolution is reached, the government must immediately initiate the proper procedure to plan the execution, deploy personnel and resources, and coordinate other departments for its implementation. Along the way, the government may still need to make some microscopic execution decisions. These decisions must faithfully follow the real intention of the resolutions. Since such decisions are only a supplement to the original resolution, their lifecycle should always be dependent on the resolution and never remain active after the execution is completed.

In addition, the government needs a mechanism of self-monitoring, information disclosure, and performance evaluation, so that citizens can accurately assess the government's works and provide feedback in a timely manner. It shall be able to discover and correct situations that concern misinterpretation of decisions, implementation delays, execution scope alterations, etc. In the case of evidently malicious power abuse, administrative and legal actions will be initiated automatically against those accountable. All of the above is the responsibility of the *Supervision Department*.

Among the above three major divisions, the supervision department holds higher independence and authority. Taking *Vianland* as an example, the government's supervision department releases monthly auditing and execution reports for all government departments. The whole people cast votes of confidence to assess each government department every quarter. If the department receives a quarterly rating below 30% or two consecutive quarterly ratings below 50%, the head of the department should be removed. For departments with a quarterly rating below 10% or two consecutive quarterly ratings below 30%, a mandatory reorganization is triggered. Under such circumstances, the removed department head shall not hold the same or higher-level posts within five years, and the reorganized department must replace no less than half of its employees.

The representative democracy system uses three branches of government (legislative, executive, and judicial) to act as the three fulcrum points of power, making them restrict each other to avoid corruption. Since the executive power is overwhelmingly strong, however, it makes this so-called "separation of powers"[1] triangle very fragile to the point that it is often crushed. However, this is nothing compared to the real problem: The most important power for democracy, the people, is missing in this design. Under the micro-democracy system, the interconnected restraints among government departments are confined to the interpretation and implementation of policies, rather than policymaking. It leaves this most important power with the people. By leveraging modern technology, micro-democracy can even divide and distribute this power across the entire population rather than as a single focal point, without compromising efficiency and stability. This infinite-fulcrum-point design has two main advantages over triangular structures:

First, it effectively prevents situations where power is manipulated by invisible forces. In many representative democratic countries, all three fulcra of power are either under the control of or bypassed by the same "shadow government." This results not only in a dysfunction of the restraint mechanism for the separation of powers but also turns it into a puppet show to divert public attention and evade accountability. Conversely, if there are infinite fulcrum points of power, they are practically impossible to bribe, intimidate, and manipulate.

Second, it simplifies the government structure and improves efficiency. The mechanism of separation of power assumes that each government branch will be under the control of different personnel. This independence is the key to form the checks and balances, but it also results in cumbersome institutions, slow processes, and expensive execution. However, if the very same force controls these three groups of people, then these added costs become meaningless. It merely brings extra social burdens and is not even as efficient as the authoritarian regimes for decision-making and execution. Contrarily, since micro-democracy achieves full decentralization of power at the citizen level, it is no longer necessary to deliberately separate government functions. As such, the government can operate in the most natural and streamlined way with improved decision-making efficiency and reduced execution costs.

To realize the authenticity and equality of the democracy, as well as many other system superiorities of micro-democracy, implementing institutional human rights is surely a core mission of the government. To serve different items under these rights, different government departments may be established, and many of them will be different from those of representative democracies.

The *Social Welfare Department* is responsible for providing citizens personal living materials according to the national standard. The standard is set through the micro-democracy procedures with domain elites of economics and public services weighted strongly. Designed to be only a basic living material supply, the standard of the supply should stay low, to discourage lazy or complacent attitudes so that it won't hurt social and economic vitality. This will also make society more resilient when facing economic downturns and natural disasters. Seeing that the standard is universal across the country, this service will not become the motivation of migration. Actually, it will reduce the situation of people being forced into exile for their livelihoods as the government aids would be no different everywhere. In addition, the standardization would help the government with the efficiency of the production, storage, transportation, and distribution of materials.

Taking *Vianland* as an example, the national standard for personal living material supply is: individual or family living space of 8 square meters per person, basic furniture and living necessities, water and electricity supply, shared kitchen and bathroom, 400 grams of daily grain supply, essential clothing, basic healthcare, electric devices with micro-democracy operation functions, unlimited data communication for accessing the micro-democracy systems and online education services, and unlimited public services phone calls.

Regarding the distribution of materials, as in *Vianland*, such benefits are only offered in administrative regions larger than 100 square kilometers with a population over 10,000. The government must deliver the benefits within 30 days of the application. If the number of new applications exceeds 10% of the local population in a month, the delivery deadline extends to 90 days. Each citizen can apply for benefits in only one location at a time. When people receive benefits in a new place, they must stop receiving similar benefits elsewhere and return the materials.

To support migration freedom, the government should facilitate the transportation and citizens' free passage across the country. But more importantly, it needs to build a citizenship information system to maintain the residency records of the people, in order to calculate the accurate voting weights for decision-making, as well as to service them with the eligible human rights benefits.

For the case of *Vianland*, migrants should register a residency change notice to the citizen information system before arrival. Along with this notice, the citizen can choose to file the application for personal living materials benefits at the destination region. Upon receiving the request, the local government must deliver the benefits within 30 days, or in case of an application surge, 90 days. This means that in order to receive the benefits upon arrival, the citizen should make this registration at least 30 days in advance. If the migrants arrive before the delivery deadline, the government should still provide some sub-standard temporary aid. Between 60 and 90 days after the migrants' reported settlement, government officials will visit the site to verify their status and confirm the actual start date of residency. On the 100th day of the confirmed residency, the migrants' record in the citizen information system will be updated and become effective officially. That is, only citizens who have lived in a region for at least 100 days are entitled to enjoy the extra relevant voting weight and local welfare human rights. To assist immigrants in adapting to the new environment, local governments should arrange some new-resident programs for them, such as monthly information briefings and seminars on local laws, regulations, and welfare.

Many of the superiorities of micro-democracy source back to the right of education: The fairness of the knowledge voting weights is attributed to unlimited equal education opportunities and unified exam standards. Professionalization of learning, combined with the personal living material benefits, guides the bottom masses along the feasible path to break class solidification and to self-upgrade. The neutral position of education opens up a broader space for society to evolve. The lifelong education and its popularization will transform the social growth model from being labor-driven to technology-driven. It is also a perfect solution to resolve the conflict between production automatization and labor employment, greatly reducing the risk of economic crises. Evidently, it is impossible to achieve all the above results by upgrading the current broken education system as there are too many gaps. A completely new type of *Education Department* is needed to fulfill all the new requirements.

First of all, the government will directly administer the design of the knowledge system and assessment standards, establish a unified discipline classification and grading system for calculating knowledge voting weights consistently. The classification of disciplines should be made accordant to their organic development, as science and culture are both progressing non-stop over time. So, whenever adjustments become necessary, the government should update the system in a timely manner and also refresh citizens' existing education records. The teaching content and assessment standards must be open and neutral, and mainstream and alternative views should be treated equally. For those contradictory theories, there can be different requirements in the depth of understanding according to their popularity and level of social adoption, but the government should not intervene in the judgment of their merits and pitfalls.

In *Vianland*, the standard curriculum for any branch of learning must include an overview course, which comprehensively introduces various and even contradictory schools and theories under this branch. Passing of this overview course is a pre-requisite for taking any follow-up course.

Second, the government will administer citizens' education degrees and teachers' qualifications throughout the country. Citizens can study in public schools, private commercial institutions, or through self-learning. In most cases, the pay for learning is calculated based on assessment results, then supplemented by the learning efforts as a minor factor. Teachers' income is calculated based on student headcount and their performance in assessments. Since learning and teaching are both considered rewardable social services and therefore part of social employment, the *Education Department* needs to integrate its grading and assessment services with the *Labor Department* and *Social Welfare Department*, in order to manage the citizens' employment benefits and social welfare under a unified framework.

In *Vianland*, when students enroll at a particular subject level, they can choose the method of learning. For students who opt for school study, the government will assign them teachers and allocate other learning resources, such as learning groups, venues, materials, and so on. Students must attend classes according to the course schedule to get paid, which is calculated based on attendance and assessment results. For students choosing self-learning, the government will also provide necessary learning resources, usually books, online courses, and lab materials. In such a case, the exam results are the only factor used to calculate their pay. A citizen who receives a grade of A in a course meets the minimal qualification to register as a teacher of that course. Therefore, a person might hold teacher status for different courses in various disciplines. There is also a rating system for teachers, primarily based on their students' recent learning results.

As learning assessments play a significant role in both economy and politics, cheating is considered a crime and will face severe consequences. The *Education Department* should work closely with the *Justice Department* to handle exam fraud and take proactive legal actions against the violators. Being a violation against an institutional human right, it may very likely be punished within the scope of institutional human rights, such as imprisonment.

Taking *Vianland* as an example, the exam propositions are confidentially prepared by top teachers. Leaking and cheating are both felonies. For non-knowledge exams, such as skill demonstrations, subjective assessments of literary and artworks, no less than five experts in the domain will preside and score. The entire process must be open to the public and recorded for future inspection.

The government and society jointly contribute the resources for educational activities. Those disciplines closely related to business activities will easily receive sponsors from the beneficiary industries. Basic scientific research and some cultural subjects will rely more on the governmental supplies. Funding for the specific high-cost education and research projects should be determined or approved through the micro-democracy process.

To protect the right to know, the government must take proactive legal action against releasing disinformation or concealing information that relates to public affairs. Besides, it should also provide the public with a trustworthy and reliable information source tracing service. These functions are managed by the *Information Department*.

The acquisition of knowledge is usually a process. As people continuously receive more information and refresh their understanding, the accuracy and completeness of their knowledge gradually improves. During this process, even if the people are subjectively honest and genuine, the information they know or deliver may still be wrong or incomplete. Historically, many once mainstream consensuses have later been proven wrong and thereafter replaced as people's knowledge and social values progressed. Therefore, people should hold an open and tolerant attitude towards every opinion and theory, even if they are contradicted. Since verifying the correctness of the information is far beyond the government's capability, no official stance should be made on it. The official information source tracking service should focus on the authenticity of information's *Original Record* rather than judging its content. The original record of information mainly includes the content, the source, and various parties' opinions on it. When there are different versions of information about the same matter, their original records must be all collected and presented to the public, even if they are contradictory. As to whether the information itself is correct, it's up to the people to draw their own conclusions independently based on their personal stance, the credibility of the information source, comments or analysis from third parties, etc. There will no longer be an "official truth" about any information— only "official original records."

Absolute truth may exist in a philosophical sense but is rare in the context of sociology, especially in politics. It only occurs when all peoples unanimously agree with a fact or opinion in the face of overwhelming evidence. This absolute truth in the social context is more of an extreme statistical case. It is entirely possible that, due to the limitation of knowledge and flaws in the evidence, the well-accepted conclusion is totally inconsistent with the absolute truth in the philosophical sense. Therefore, democratic decision-making based on absolute truth is next to impossible. However, with the comprehensive original records of information, people will get closer to the absolute truth, and to the greatest extent, mitigate the influences of subjective maliciousness and objective limitations of information sources.

To deliver the above functions, the government will use large scale databases to collect, store, and maintain all available original records of information, provide indexing and querying services to the public at no cost. The "facts" stated in many sources of information depend on other facts being true. For example, "the moon affects the tides," is a statement that relies on many other facts, such as "the moon orbits the earth," "theory of gravity," "patterns of the tides," and so on. The extended information traceability service can thereby present such inherent relevance of information. The system can also extend the information source elements to reveal the people who provided additional supporting evidence and endorsement, so that in judging the facts, citizens can further consider the credibility of these endorsers.

Fighting for resources and interests is nothing new, and unfortunately this struggle still holds the center stage of modern international relations. Confrontational state relations are inevitably strongly dependent on military power. Peace between countries is not necessarily a product of friendly ties, but often the balance of force and deterrence, which is temporary and very fragile. On the contrary, the world order of micro-democracy does not need this precarious balance to operate. The primary interaction among micro-democracy countries is not confrontation and competition but integration, for they are sharing mutual goals. Although in an ideal world of micro-democracy, the military presence is unnecessary, in the process of its emergence and growth, micro-democracy nations have to coexist with modern states which will be hostile to this new system for an extended period. So, at least for the early years, micro-democracy still needs the *Defense Department.*

Sadly, even military forces built for legitimate self-defense purposes will still pose a threat to the micro-democracy system itself. This is because a certain degree of arbitrariness and confidentiality in the military operations can help the nation to most effectively fight external threats. While a practical need, this nonetheless represents a violation of institutional human rights, and thus would corrode the foundation of micro-democracy. The micro-democracy government should consciously limit the military influence within the minimum necessary scope and take active institutional measures to keep military forces from unnecessary expansion.

For extreme cases like wars, natural disasters, or the destruction of infrastructure, it may be necessary for the military to take over the nation operation temporarily through martial law, making the country respond to the crisis more efficiently. But in the meantime, these measures will suspend the micro-democracy operation and push the nation back to a state of autocracy and authority. Therefore, specific mechanisms are needed (at the level of system structure and laws) to ensure that the government automatically resume micro-democracy status as soon as the crisis ends.

In *Vianland*, there are always three independent military commanding groups standing by. The first group consists of active-duty personnel, and the other two are retired veterans. Normally, the first group leads the military, and only they can initiate the national military emergency. If the micro-democracy system is still functioning, such military emergencies require approvals from a referendum as temporary law. Without proper legal authorization, the troops should refuse the command of the above group to execute missions under the emergency law and take necessary action to restore the normal social order. During an authorized emergency, the micro-democracy decision-making mechanism is temporarily suspended. The military's priority is to resolve the crisis and restore the nation back to the normal micro-democracy state as soon as possible. Such a military emergency lasts for a maximum of 120 days and ends automatically. If an extension is needed, it should still be approved by a referendum, unless the micro-democracy function has not resumed. Regardless of how it's extended, the maximum extension is still 120 days, and commanding power must be transferred from the current leadership group to the next group in the queue within 20 days. On the deadline, the previous group loses its authority and is dismissed automatically, and the next group will take over. Three groups take turns commanding in the event of multiple extensions of the military emergency. The group that finishes its turn must dismiss and then reorganize within 60 days. The reorganized group should have no less than 50% of new members who are not from the active-duty personnel.

Reverting from wartime to normal micro-democracy is a process, and the most critical step is the full disclosure of information. The importance of confidentiality to military operations causes the right to know often to be the first institutional human right taken away from people in wartime. But revealing the truth is equally vital for micro-democracy in peacetime. So, it is the top priority for restoring the system, as it prevents conspirators from stealing the country under the name of emergencies.

Taking *Vianland* as an example, with authorization from a referendum, the government can implement temporary information confidentiality for up to 120 days under a military emergency. Only information about military operations, personnel, production and transportation of military supplies can be classified as confidential. After the military emergency ends, the confidential information will be gradually declassified: At least 50% of them must be declassified within 120 days, no less than 80% must be declassified within one year, and declassification of all information must be completed within two years.

As the final line of defense, soldiers must be loyal to micro-democracy systems, treat them as the highest code of conduct, and prioritize them over orders from superior commanders. No matter what excuse the high-ranking military leaders use to undermine the principle of micro-democracy, every soldier is obligated to disobey and resist any attempts to restore authoritarian regimes.

In addition to the core government departments closely related to the micro-democracy system as mentioned above, some other administrative and technical departments are also needed to support the operation of the whole country, such as the *Transportation*

Department, the *Agriculture Department*, the *Energy Department*, the *Commerce Department*, the *Healthcare Department*, and so on. Although these departments do not have the unique characteristics of micro-democracy, they are still an indispensable part of the national government system.

 # World

Micro-democracy will reshape the world. It starts with a simple premise: to give local residents the decision-making power on local affairs and to protect the freedom of migration as a universal institutional human right. This combination positions micro-democracy to naturally oppose the national borders or any artificial political ruling boundaries. Imagine a situation in which the borderline of two adjacent micro-democracy countries cuts through a natural habitat area of people, with residents living on either side of the border belonging to the different voting weight systems. In such a case, decisions made on one side of the border would ignore or downplay the voice of the residents living on the other side, even though the decision would affect both. The interests and time relevance principles of the micro-democracy voting rules are thus broken, causing inequality between people living near the border. Only by removing such artificial boundaries, matching the administrative areas with people's actual habitat areas, and applying micro-democracy to local affairs decision-making in a consistent way can such inequality be eliminated. To micro-democracy countries, the only right thing to do is for the two countries to actually merge into one. Due to this tendency of natural converging, even if multiple micro-democracy countries may co-exist temporarily during their formation and development, they will eventually join into a unified micro-democracy world. By then, the modern nation will have completed its historic mission, and the world will become borderless and as one.

This unified micro-democracy world is fundamentally different from the notion of today's globalization and world government.

First, the micro-democracy world runs on a self-operated, decentralized, purely technical framework, not taking direction from a central authority of any sort. The vast majority of decisions are made directly by local people in a self-governing manner in regions of various levels. Even global policies are initiated by the public through a bottom-up process and made by direct participation of all the citizens, unlike in the so-called globalized world government system, where elite politicians, political parties, and administrative bureaucrats rule the people top-down unilaterally with overwhelming force from central governments. In the micro-democracy world, such players only serve as auxiliary roles in a dynamic manner and are not even part of the government. From a macro perspective, the micro-democracy government is not a centralized decision-making center but a service provider.

Second, the micro-democracy world respects regional autonomy and welcomes social diversity, providing an inclusive environment for different groups and cultures to coexist and compete. This is achieved with the combination of migration freedom and additional voting weights. When policies in a region are more effective for economics and more inspiring for cultures, that region will naturally attract populations from other areas, becoming a role model to other regions. As a result, better policies will expand to larger areas and people, winning the peaceful competition of social evolution. Nevertheless, those non-mainstream social forms do not have to go extinct; groups of special cultures can always find an undisturbed place to settle down and gain the advantage of decisions on their land. Thus, experimental social forms can still persist in their own autonomous space, creating their unique laws and regulations according to micro-democracy rules, and continue to evolve.

Globalization movements and the world governments are pushing for a unitary social form as their solution to resolve social conflicts, which is the opposite of the idea of local self-determination and social diversity. When the elites impose on the people so-called superior social structures and world order they designed, they curb the development space of civilization, strangling its vitality. Furthermore, as the economic enslavement of the masses strengthens, social conflicts will constantly escalate and intensify, leading to a police state reliant on an iron hand to rule, which in turn will eventually be destroyed by the fiery resistance of the oppressed.

Modern nations have an intense appetite for territory. They never miss a chance to occupy any space they can reach that others have not taken. When strength allows, they never hesitate to turn the calm land and waters into bloody battlefields. History is the primary source of their territorial claims, which they typically use to suggest that they are entitled to inherit a piece of land from their glorious ancestors. However, most of the lands have been occupied and ruled alternately by different nations, religions, and empires throughout history, so such excuses lead to nowhere but endless conflicts. In fact, many disputed territories are uninhabitable—only distant barren lands or remote waters—yet people from different countries are sadly turned into enemies over their ownership. Of course, the inhabited fertile land invites only more misery. But in many cases, the tragedy is imposed on the helpless local residents, while the glory and profits are reserved for the rulers and special interest groups. In some cases, there are leaders who sincerely believe that for the well-being and honor of the nation, religion, or race, it is a noble cause to expand the country's territory as much as possible. Unfortunately, this ambition is akin to apes fighting for space on branches, primitive tribes grabbing hunting grounds, or ancient nations keeping slaves and plundering. It represents an outdated, backward, and rather barbaric old culture. In the coming era of the demise of modern countries, this kind of fighting is pathetic and childish.

Fights for territory will come to an end in the world of micro-democracy. The voting weight rule will enable only the residents living on the land to be its real owners. Anybody else wanting to have a say over and profit from the land must move and live there, earning the voting weights honestly with their time of life. And those uninhabited lands and waters are not subject to nor need supervision from the government. After all, any governance can only be carried out through the administration by the people. The world of micro-democracy encourages people to move to and settle down in those inaccessible places and build new cultures and society as they wish, as long as they respect all the institutional human rights and are friendly to the future newcomers. Once the population and living time of the residents meet the administrative division standards, the micro-democracy world will automatically grant them the voting weight on local affairs. From here on, they can manage local affairs and practice autonomy within the framework of micro-democracy. When some areas no longer meet the standards due to population decline, the region will delist from the micro-democracy governance system and be regarded as a desolate land again.

For example, in *Vianland*, when 1,000 people continuously live within an area of a radius of 50 kilometers for more than one year, an administrative region should be set up. Government offices will be established to provide institutional human rights, and the region profile will be created in the micro-democracy information system. When a region no longer meets standards, for example, when fewer than 500 people have lived within an area of a radius of 50 kilometers for three consecutive years, the administrative region will be delisted or merged into adjacent regions.

It is entirely feasible to transform modern nations into micro-democracy countries peacefully, and to eventually merge them into one micro-democracy world. Still, it cannot be ruled out, that the micro-democracy world may have to end the era of the modern states through war.

War is by no means the preferred path to the micro-democracy world. The structure of modern states has inherent infrastructure for war mobilization, but these wartime measures are utterly harmful to the micro-democracy countries. The micro-democracy countries' critical infrastructure is vulnerable during war, and their hallmark decision-making mechanisms must be temporarily suspended for efficient operations. Even if it wins a long-fought war, a once micro-democratic country might become a de facto modern state due to a failure to restore the micro-democracy rules. Therefore, war imposes both internal and external threats to the micro-democracy system.

Despite facing disadvantages in war, micro-democracy has the upper hand in conducting a peaceful evolution of modern states. This is because even without the government structure, people can still practice micro-democracy, as long as the purpose of decision-making is to serve the majority and to pursue higher decision quality compared to the one-person-one-vote rule. It means people can explore, experience, and improve micro-democracy, even within modern states. Once people have become accustomed to this method and recognize its superiority, they will naturally demand to upgrade the political operation with the micro-democracy principles. After all, the notion of micro-democracy is fundamentally consistent with the democratic concepts claimed by modern states, except for some key optimizations. After micro-democracy procedural improvements are introduced, the significance of the institutional human rights will become more apparent, for they help decision-making become not only wise but also fair and equal. With the institutional human rights of the micro-democracy system realized as well, the transformation from a modern state to a micro-democracy country is virtually complete.

Undoubtedly, politicians and special interest groups of modern states will use state machines to obstruct and prohibit people from practicing micro-democracy or destroy the newborn micro-democracy countries with wars. But in this world-scale fight between the two camps, the victory will be with micro-democracy. This is because micro-democracy disintegrates hostile forces from within, naturally and comprehensively. When the people of modern states begin to practice micro-democracy spontaneously, the force to suppress micro-democracy will gradually weaken and even vanish by itself. If this process is smooth enough, the transformation from modern states into micro-democracy may be completed in peace. But if the enemies amass their force early enough, then people may have to go through the hard time of internal oppression and external wars and fight all the way to the world of micro-democracy. It is even possible that the rulers of modern states would collude with all other non-democratic, centralized regimes to form a global alliance against micro-democracy to extinguish the common threat. However, micro-democracy is their unbeatable enemy. The more fiercely they fight micro-democracy, the faster and deeper the people of modern states will learn about micro-democracy, and the more they will think and compare it with the status quo. As such, seeds of peaceful evolution of micro-democracy will be spread and rooted under the ground of modern states. Even if the micro-democracy countries are defeated in the battlefields, or even temporarily destroyed, those seeds will still sprout and flourish in suitable soils. The ultimate victory of micro-democracy will occur in peoples' hearts, rather than on the battleground.

Profound changes will come to the economic domain as well. Personal property is divided into categories under personal belongings and personal assets. They are put separately under the coverage of the institutional human rights and welfare human rights, and correspondingly, protected by the micro-democracy constitution or regional common laws.

People can earn passive income from their assets, which in truth is exploiting the labor value of others, directly or indirectly. Communist movements deem such exploitation as being morally evil and necessary to be eliminated. However, in practice, without a definite distinction between personal belongings and personal assets, it often ends up affecting all the personal properties, which severely violates fundamental human rights, and sometimes even threatens people's survival. In a capitalist society, this exploitation is precisely the intrinsic driving force that stimulates economic activities. It is a beneficial and necessary evil that must be exceptionally protected. The consequence is sharp social division—a world of the rich enslaving over the poor.

Unlike any previous polity and mainstream political theory, for micro-democracy, the economic and political systems do not have to be integrated and interdependent. Decoupling these two kinds of systems is not only a possibility but also a necessity. Doing so makes the micro-democracy system more inclusive and vital. Whether to protect personal assets for promoting social production or to ignore it for eliminating exploitation, is essentially more of an economic issue than a political one. As for how to balance social justice and material production efficiency, the micro-democracy system leaves this to the local people to decide through making regional common laws.

As the relevant voting weights for deciding regional affairs are given to the actual residents only, owning assets in the region does not always bring political power to the rich who live elsewhere. Therefore, the economic influence of capital can only be exerted on politics indirectly through the residents, rather than directly overriding the will of the local people.

The original intention for the new education system design is for citizens to have equal opportunities to earn the extra voting weights, but its effects on the economy model are even more significant.

Education will no longer only be the learning and teaching of civic literacy and vocational skills for the young, but a social service and lifelong career everybody can engage in. As no one can master all the knowledge and skills in his or her lifetime, the openings for the job of learning are infinite; accordingly, the demand for the teachers will be massive too. Under any circumstances, people can always choose to learn something new and earn income, so passive unemployment will disappear forever.

Even if the pay for learning jobs is low, it will still draw many primary workers, causing severe labor shortages for the manufacturing and service industries. The wages for these industries will raise, and consequently, so will the commodity prices. This pricing trend will route automation, robotics, artificial intelligence technologies to the low-end positions where most of the workforce is released. Usually, such positions are the least desired jobs like heavy manual labors and repetitive works which people are only forced into for their livelihoods. These replaced jobs produced less happiness than the learning ones; thus, such transformation will directly improve social utility. At the same time, this transformation will upgrade the economy from being value-oriented to intelligence-oriented.

The so-called value-oriented economy means that the primary goal of investments of capital, materials, and technology aim for the maximum return through commodity or service sales. Since the Return of Investment (ROI)[1] is its primary Key Performance Indicator (KPI)[2], the production of goods and the provision of services are all to serve the needs of those with higher spending power, and most value returns to the investors who happen to be the same high spending people. These people both consume the best of products of the labor and receive the most profits so that they can consume even more. It's fair to conclude this economic model is essentially is the vast number of poor people serving the few rich. Ultimately, this contradiction between maximizing return on investment and maximizing the overall happiness of people (that is, social utility) results in a sharp social polarization, worship of wealth, and corruption of human nature.

The technology capable of replacing those manual and repetitive low-income jobs has been around for a long time and is mature. It is the low return of investment that prevents it from being applied in these areas. For the same reason, it is more likely those high-income, high-skill, and high-education jobs that are to be replaced. As such, technology is destroying rather than encouraging education and knowledge. The new education system in micro-democracy will turn this situation around. While providing low-skilled workers with more attractive career choices, improving their knowledge and professional level, it will dramatically reduce the labor supply of those low-income jobs and cause the salary to rise. This dynamic makes it profitable to automate low-end works with technology, giving back high-skill and high-intelligent posts to humans.

This approach may raise a concern: Whether the withdrawal of massive laborers from the manufacturing and service industries will cause a sharp decline in social production output and shortages of materials, affecting people's living standards? It might sound counter-intuitive, but the excessive labor force often drops productivity. Too much workforce makes labor cheap, and cheap labor puts high-tech machinery into a disadvantage under the measurements of return of investment, blocking the application of technology. On the contrary, the shortage of labor will actually encourage the use of technology and eventually increase output.[3] This principle has been proven in agriculture production: In countries lacking farming labors, large-scale machinery production is easier to achieve and form economies of scale. In traditional agricultural countries with a large peasant population, the government hesitates to promote scale production as it would threaten the livelihood of those peasants, so that technology cannot be fully utilized, and therefore the agriculture output remains low. If the education industry can absorb most of the agricultural labor, then the biggest obstacles to large-scale mechanization and high-tech production in these countries will be removed, and eventually, agricultural production will increase. The same situation happens in the industrial production and service sector.

As the above approach is promoted to the entire economy, the new intelligence-oriented economy will take shape. To the greatest extent, it frees people from low-end heavy manual and repetitive work, so that they can upgrade to become mental workers and contribute more to the economy and society, and also live a better life. As such, brainpower is released by technology from the domain in which it was most undervalued. Through this path, technology will bring the huge human intellectual resource into economic activities, with the highest cost performance.

The new intelligence-oriented economy is not only good for optimizing social resources allocation and maximizing the happiness of working people. More importantly, it is the grandest strategic investment for the development of human civilization. A plethora of instances have shown that even a handful of technology breakthroughs may bring about incredible value to society, be it reducing labor intensity, increasing life expectancy, or raising living standards. Such astonishing achievements have happened in a time when there were very few people who had the luxury to attend high-level education and access scientific research resources. There are reasons to believe that the micro-democracy education system will increase the overall human brainpower investment in research, invention, and creativity exponentially, explosively intensify the progress of science and culture, and revolutionize production technology. The returns will be more than sufficient to offset the reduction of the workforce that engages in direct production, which will also significantly improve people's life quality. In the new age, there will still be people working, but their primary motivation will no longer be making a living, but the pursuit of social responsibility, a sense of achievement, and honor. In the not-too-distant future, humans will be able to automate the entire social production, enabling people to fully devote themselves to learning, creating and enjoying life.

The micro-democracy government is the primary employer of the education industry and scientific research, and accordingly owns the intellectual property created from the educational and scientific research activities. Since the micro-democracy government belongs to the people, these intellectual properties also belong to the people and can be freely used by the entire society at no cost. The situation in which a lot of human intellectual achievements are sealed as patents and cannot contribute to the world will be no more. As a special kind of asset, intellectual property is not part of institutional human rights; therefore, it is not protected by the micro-democracy constitution or national laws in the global scope. Each administrative region can determine whether and how to protect it with regional laws, but these laws only apply locally. Due to the unique nature of knowledge and information, it easily flows across regions, so the strictly exclusive authorization and use of knowledge are sometimes impractical. Obviously, this will change the way companies invest in scientific research, making cross-enterprise collaborative studies more common. Duplicated research works by separate corporations will be reduced, sparing more brainpower for more advanced and original technology research.

This economic model transformation will eventually be a matter of life or death for humanity. When the obsession of return of investments, or value, pushes the economy to the extreme, it often ends up with the military-industrial complex intruding into and controlling the economy, a nasty and devastating ultimate stage. When the value-oriented economy evolves to its highest stage, even excessive consumption will tend to be saturated, and growth runs into its limit and is no longer sustainable. Economic oligarchs must find and create new demands. The construction of large-scale public utilities and the manufacturing of military equipment are the two primary solutions. The non-transparency and exclusivity of the arms business make it much more profitable than the former, because as the money flows in directly from government funding, it becomes the favorite of economic oligarchs. When the military, weapon manufacturing enterprises, and politicians collude, the monster of the military-industrial complex is born: It manipulates the troops or terrorist organizations to provoke military conflicts and then consumes the weaponry and equipment. All these costs are either paid by every citizen as tax or collected from the defeated countries as a ransom. The money eventually flows to the military-industrial complex in the name of national security and world order. At that moment, the sin of the value-oriented economy is far beyond exploiting workers, over-extracting natural resources, or destroying the natural environment. It is a demon slaughtering the innocents, a generator of humanitarian disasters, and ultimately it poses a direct threat to the survival of humanity.

Losing the power they once held is intolerable to politicians, political parties, and special interest groups. They will do everything in their ability to maintain, consolidate, and permanently occupy the power tightly in their hands. With their advantageous position and strength, it is relatively easy for those in power to create a social environment in their favor, suppress rivals, and eliminate any possible threats. Dictators of autocratic and authoritarian regimes prefer open intimidation with force, while those in so-called democracies are better at exploiting loopholes in laws and procedures, kidnapping public opinion, and abusing judicial authority to strengthen power.

In the new world, the old decaying political vices will have no place to stay but the trash can of history. Since no individual or political force under the micro-democracy system can hold power steadily and exclusively, there is no point in maintaining, consolidating, and occupying it. The only lasting existence is the neutral political machine, which includes the information system and infrastructure for micro-democracy decision-making, and the constitutional laws to support its normal functions. The former is comparable to the hardware of a computer, while the latter plays a similar role as the operating system that runs with the hardware. Just like the modern computer, it has the potential to do countless tasks, which are all done by other software running on the hardware and operating system. The memory space running this "other software" can be likened to the administrative regions organically formed in the micro-democracy world. The functions performed by this "other software" can be likened to the external behaviors directed by democratic decision-making. Just like the ecosystem where many types of software can simultaneously run in the modern computer, countless designers and developers created them, and they can perform a variety of tasks, many far exceeding the imagination of the inventors of computers and operating systems. Similarly, the micro-democracy system runs as an open platform for the development of human civilization. The institutional human rights it protects are only for the continuous operation of the platform and to ensure the social forms developed on it are constructive, protective, and safe, not self-destructive. Based on this most basic premise, it is conceivable that various societies will emerge on this platform, peacefully compete in this safe environment, and continuously evolve into better social forms through non-violent natural selection. Those more diverse and superior future social forms evolved on this platform may far exceed the imagination of the authors and readers of this book today. However, we can still choose to become the greatest dreamer of this era and lay the most solid foundation for the new world.

 Road

The road to the world of micro-democracy is full of hope and challenges, beginning with the awareness of new choices in building a different society.

After the bloody fight of the World Wars and the standoff of the Cold War, people finally welcomed the victory of democracy and freedom, but social justice and happiness did not follow as expected. With the ideological rivals defeated, the ruling groups no longer bothered to whitewash their manipulation of politics and despise of public opinion. So, people could finally see that the rituals of democracy were only special interest groups' power plays, while the general public were just props, tools, and weapons of the game. Under the seemingly noble cover, the globalization movement has only one true master: the special interest groups. Its real function is a trading platform for elites and flowing capitals to hunt for high-grade exploitation prey worldwide. Humanity is in desperate need of a new breakthrough, but people were told that they had gotten the best system, and that was the "end of history"[1]. Disappointed and furious, people turned to the old world's toolbox in search of any possible antidote. Totalitarianism, nationalism, and extreme religions, like half-buried ghosts, emerged from their graves once again, chanting to people in the darkness.

Now the most pressing priority is to announce the birth of this brand-new form of democracy, showing people that the new idea is not only appealing but also practical. Creating a new country directly or taking over an existing one to implement micro-democracy is not as simple as it sounds. A more viable path would be that people first find suitable scenarios and apply micro-democracy in their daily life. After becoming familiar with, used to, and respectful of this new method, they can progressively expand its application scope until finally upgrading the political system of the country.

The initial implementation will be much simpler than it has to be for the national level. Due to the absence of some core features such as laws, human rights, and the administrative region lifecycle, it cannot provide sufficient equality as designed in micro-democracy. Even so, it will still significantly improve decision quality and social utility. This simplification also makes it easy to implement; a small or medium-sized software team could build it within weeks. As a matter of fact, even for a national scale full-function micro-democracy system, there's no insurmountable technical difficulty. The complexity of such a system is similar to that of large social platforms or banking systems, and many big information technology companies are adequate for these kinds of projects.

The truth is, the real obstacle standing in the way to micro-democracy is not technology. People are the key factor. According to the theory of Dialectic and Historical Materialism[2], every revolution that promotes social progress has its main force led by the group that represents the advanced productivity and production relations. Just like the 19th-century European democratic revolution was achieved by free citizens led by the emerging industrial and commercial capital classes[3], the 20th-century communist revolutions in Russia and China were achieved by the peasants led by the emerging worker class[4]. It is not difficult to infer that only those who have the knowledge and ability to build a micro-democratic system could become the pioneers of this revolution. The information workers are precisely the emerging group who have mastered this most advanced productivity and know-how. Like they have radically changed people's lives in the domain of economy, only they can show people the power and potential of technology and stimulate new demands in political life. Attracted by the new theory, other workers who became familiar with and adapted to the digital lifestyle and the free citizens with exploratory spirits will together form the core force of the micro-democratic movement.

Additionally, it is imperative to identify the allies and enemies of micro-democracy:

Internationalists are allies of micro-democracy. Internationalism and globalization share some similarities, and both had broad influences. Like these two theories, micro-democracy also proposes a globally integrated political system, but its core idea is much different.

Internationalism was the supranational ideology of the communist movement based on class theory. It placed great emphasis on classes' differences and the contradictions among them, as well as the decisive role of economic relations in politics. Although the micro-democracy world is supranational as well, it is class-neutral and not binding to any specific economic relation.

Globalization was the global political-economic integration movement led by international capitals. It aimed at a global market and economic integration and helped the transnational capital to access more resources and surplus value. Therefore, in its implementation, the priority was to satisfy the capitals' pursuit of profit. Its accompanying political system, social justice, and cultural development are all only secondary issues and instruments that can all be sacrificed and ignored as long as the capital's desire for market integration is fulfilled and the environments are profit friendly. On the contrary, micro-democracy is mainly a political system that gives priority to social utility, neither relying on nor pursuing global economic integration.

Obviously, the fundamental difference between micro-democracy and the above two is its neutral attitude towards economic models, as it is entirely a political framework rather than an economical one. Although its implementation will inevitably interact with and impose broad influence over economic activities and relations, this link still remains loose and open. The most direct proof is that it allows different regions in a country to design different economic models and policies autonomously. The national laws only protect personal belongings and the seriousness of contracts. The formulation of all other economic rules and regulations is considered within the scope of regional laws. Consequently, each region can decide those fundamental issues related to the economic models itself, such as the ownership of personal assets and its incidental rights, as long as they do not violate any institutional human rights. This openness makes it possible for different economic models to operate independently, evolve, and compete amicably in various regions. The result of its competition is not the regime changes, but the expansion, contraction, merging, and evolution among regions with contrasting economic models.

Despite all the differences, micro-democracy still shares many visions with these two movements, such as its will to achieve unification of the world in some way, and to eliminate the division, isolation, conflict, and even war caused by national, religious, and economic systems, so that people may live in a safer, more equal, and more harmonious world. It is probably not the real purpose and primary motivation of the leaders of the two movements, but it is likely to be the goal and ideal of many, even most, of their advocates and participants. Therefore, if micro-democracy provides a superior solution for this ideal, then these genuine and passionate internationalists may well be drawn to it and become the backbone of the micro-democracy revolution.

Laborers are allies of micro-democracy. With institutional human rights, the majority of workers will have the conditions to escape from heavy labor, engage in higher-value activities, and enjoy a more comfortable and dignified life.

Karl Marx once pointed out that the profits for capitalists mainly come from the surplus value of productive labor.[5] Without hiring, capitalists have nothing to exploit and their capital loses the ability to grow. Therefore, increasing jobs and production must be the goal that capitalists desperately pursue. With cleverly designed social welfare systems, economic theory, and public opinion, they successfully implanted this selfish goal into the public's "common sense" and made it laborers' fundamental need. Hence, the maximization of employment and market scale has become akin to religious worship in the modern market economy.

The truth is that with the application of automation, today's technologies are already capable of serving all people's needs of living, with a significantly reduced workforce. At the same time, social production has not only far exceeded a necessary level but has also been adequate to provide people with better working conditions, to enjoy less labor time, extra spare time, and a more relaxed lifestyle. Since this outcome is not in favor of capitalists, they adopted three countermeasures to avoid such a situation: the first promoted consumerism and stimulated people's demand for goods and services. When there is no demand, they will manage to create a social atmosphere that encourages over-consumption and overproduction. Clearly, this approach is unsustainable; eventually, it will exhaust the planet's natural resources and destroy the planet's ecological environment. The second countermeasure was to increase the demand for the service sector. When the production of material merchandise has far exceeded people's needs, massive non-material services are invented, attracting or forcing people to "enjoy." Of course, people will have to exchange these services with even more hard work. By growing the service sector, capitalists not only enjoy a better life at lower prices but also extract more surplus value from workers through these services. The third countermeasure was to find a new social welfare basin in the process of globalization and use it to pull down the welfare level in other regions. For capitalists, this has double benefits: On the one hand, it allows more material resources to enter the capital market rather than the public welfare domain, which gives the capital more leverage. On the other hand, more people are forced into the labor market, generating value for the capitalist under the employment relationship.

Facing the above problems, micro-democracy doesn't simply take a position to oppose capitalism and the market economy like some other social movements. Despite severe flaws in the status quo, it is unwise to disrupt existing systems when there is not yet an ideal alternative. However, without touching upon the problem's roots, it is also impossible to produce substantive results by making minor corrections. Micro-democracy's solution to this problem is the personal living materials supply and the education system. It gives workers, especially those at the bottom, a truly viable path to choose and change their lives, providing them a material basis for getting rid of the economic chains that constrain personal freedom. Under this system, workers gain a stronger position in the negotiation with capitalists, which will significantly improve their working conditions, compensation, and social status. People will no longer be coerced into work but will make a personal choice to enhance their quality of life and realize self-value. As a result, workers will surely become close allies with micro-democracy and become the new system's most potent source of power.

Liberals are natural allies of micro-democracy. Liberalism values peoples' self-selection and self-governance, but such choices are under strict suppression in modern states, and democratic ones are no exception. This is because the politicians and ruling groups need to lock and guard their vested interests. Additionally, there is no mechanism in existing political systems to truly implement dynamic autonomy. In such a case, people can only resort to exceptional means to fight for their self-governance. Inevitably this causes tension and confrontation between social groups, escalating all the way to violent conflict, social unrest and humanitarian disaster. In most cases, it does not end with autonomy; even if it does, the political arrangements were often more based on the balance of armed force rather than accurately reflecting public opinion. What's more, whether or not it reached a fair, reasonable, and welcomed self-government solution at the time, the solidification of such a solution was just another new hurdle for posterity.

Regional autonomy is built into the routine process of the micro-democracy system and can be initiated any time from any level in a peaceful and orderly manner. This flexibility enables the division of administrative regions and the formulation of laws to constantly respond to the people's wishes. By implementing resolution amendments and automated re-validation, dynamic autonomy will be the norm. People no longer need to take aggressive action only for locking-in specific arrangements once and forever, resulting in greater social harmony.

The implementation of autonomy in micro-democracy is not only broadened geographically, increasing the population base, but also has a broader applicable scope. This means that people can decide on much more regarding public affairs and have much more control over their life. Except for the very limited institutional human rights that are protected by the constitution, many of the subjects restricted nowadays, such as welfare human rights, economic models, social rules, etc., will be open for citizens to decide in the new system. The expansion of the right of citizens to autonomy has accordingly reduced the government's authority space. It is in line with liberalism's notion of the society of small government.

However, between liberalism and micro-democracy there are obvious disparities in their views of personal property. To liberalism, people's rights to personal property are divine and must be strictly protected. To micro-democracy, this is conditional and limited as traditional personal property is subdivided into personal belongings and personal assets. The former is strictly and unconditionally protected as part of institutional human rights, while the latter is adjustable under welfare human rights and economic models, and thus is open to the public to regulate in regional laws. In this sense, micro-democracy is not a pure liberal system. Nevertheless, with the decision-making mechanism and the legal structure in micro-democracy, liberals can still legislate regional laws to provide more significant and extensive protection for personal property and can build a liberalism-oriented society in certain regions. If such a community is superior enough, naturally, it will spread to a larger area and population. And this peaceful social competition mechanism is by itself a tribute to the higher-level notions of liberalism.

Compared to liberalism, progressivism is an even closer ally of micro-democracy. The consensus of liberalism and micro-democracy is in design thinking, the point of convergence of progressivism and micro-democracy is in core values: maximizing the overall happiness of the entire people, increasing the utility of society, which is considered the ultimate goal of all political activities. In this sense, micro-democracy can even be seen as an advanced version of progressivism.

Micro-democracy meets progressivism's core pursuit of civil rights and benefits by protecting institutional human rights. It also endows the local residents with the power to define welfare human rights that adapt to specific situations in the area. The dynamic administrative region mechanism perfectly addresses the issues for implementing welfare policies in the current state structure. This unified nationwide standard is hard to meet the diverse needs of different regions and groups, and the vast scale also makes it very challenging to implement. By allowing individual areas and groups to build the social operation method that best meets their wishes, micro-democracy not only reduces the difficulty of implementation but also fulfills the unique needs of each group, and therefore the social utility level is raised from the nation's lower line to each region's upper line.

The regional autonomy mechanism creates open spaces for people and social groups to design new social forms, without any constraints of particular economic models, social codes, or welfare standards. In this way, unlike any existing government and superstructure, a micro-democratic society can grow unbound forever without limiting itself.

The distinction of personal belongings and personal assets opens a door for people to innovate economy models, which will help reconcile the adversary between commercial interests and social utility. Over time, people will find an ideal balance between economic development, public welfare, and environmental protection.

Of course, the new education system contributes greatly to improve people's working conditions, as well as the development of society. The tremendous increase in human resources in science, technology, and culture has expanded the space for social evolution and has hastened the pace of social progress, bringing the advancement of human civilization towards another climax.

Micro-democracy is against oppression and war, and it promotes the integration among social groups and ideas as well as their peaceful competition. But what makes it exceptional is that, beyond goodwill, it comes with a practical solution that works. It is no wonder that pacifists will become allies of micro-democracy.

The interpretations of the nature and roots of wars vary from different perspectives. From the micro-democracy viewpoint, there are two leading causes of wars between modern nations. One root cause is the lust for power on the part of the rulers or ruling groups. To maintain and expand power, fulfill the personal sense of mission, honor, and the duty of acquiring more benefits for the collective (or put another way: ambition, vanity, and greed), they will not hesitate to use deadly force at the expense of people's lives and happiness. Because the ruler or ruling group has tremendous institutional and economic resources to manipulate the law and control media, these motives can be easily disguised by being spun into a lofty mission, fooling the brave and decent people. But to make this approach more effective, it is necessary to combine the second cause: isolation. As the gap between people grows deeper and wider, it becomes easier for rulers to provoke contradictions, then arouse disgust and hatred between the people. To make this happen, countries and borders are essential instruments, and this includes geographic and physical barriers, as well as information and language isolation. When people lack the channels and capabilities to communicate directly and share common life experiences, the manipulation of media and public opinion can achieve the most devastating effects. A common phenomenon today is that people between the two countries can transform from friendly to disgusting and even become extremely hostile to each other, with a few carefully arranged isolated incidents and artificially engineered public opinions. Although the people in the two countries have not changed their lifestyle and behaviors before and after these incidents, and the incidents themselves may not impact people's lives at all, people can still develop a deep hatred towards each other, sometimes leading to killings. When cooperation becomes useful for these rulers, with their machines of media and public opinion, they can quickly reverse the atmosphere of the whole society and make people befriend each other again. The victims of the war are forgotten until the rulers need their tragedy to incubate new hatred and provoke the next conflict. Ridiculous, sad, and shameful as this is, it is still a reality staged in this world every day.

Under the micro-democracy system, both these roots of war will be weakened and eliminated. Firstly, rulers and ruling groups no longer exist in the political structure, and the will to power of these privileged individuals and groups will lose its breeding ground. Advocates of war will still exist, but without the monopoly laws and control of information, they cannot overwhelm people with a single voice and suppress those callings for peace. People will be able to learn about the situation from a more rational, balanced, and constructive perspectives. Misunderstandings and confrontations can be expeditiously resolved and reconciled, reducing the risk of war. Secondly, with the development of modern communication and transportation technologies, as well as the migration freedom, the interregional integration of people can occur continuously, making it harder for exclusive and antagonistic groups to take shape. Besides, because decisions can more accurately reflect the will of the people and be made dynamically in terms of time and space, it becomes easier for disputes to reach a fair and balanced settlement sooner. Even if some unjust resolutions and regulations were formed through violence, they couldn't last long, and therefore will turn out meaningless. Consequently, the chance of violent interregional conflicts within micro-democracy countries or wars between micro-democracy countries is exceptionally faint, if not non-existent.

Of course, the possibility of wars between micro-democratic and non-micro-democratic countries indeed exists. However, the natural pacifist tendency of the micro-democracy and its high vigilance against the institutional risks of war mobilization mechanisms makes it almost impossible for a pure micro-democratic country to provoke conflicts and wars proactively; it can only to respond to wars for self-defense.

There is a view that the scarcity of resources and population growth causes an eternal contradiction that makes conflict and war inevitable. In fact, only improving the production and utilization of resources, not destroying and killing, can grow material wealth and resolve this contradiction fundamentally. Natural resources are not unlimited, but the potential of science and technology is. As long as sufficient investment of manpower is continuously poured into scientific research on the development of efficient use of resources, there are good reasons to believe that human civilization can sustainably develop without exhausting resources and living space. However, another cause of the resource shortage is greed in people's hearts. Under its influence, people indulge in the desire for material things, become wasteful, and addicted to possession. The source of these bad habits comes from human suffering that has played out over thousands of years. These miseries are etched into all aspects of human culture, affecting people's beliefs and behaviors, often leading to more suffering in turn. It is not simple to get rid of this vicious circle, nor can it be resolved overnight. However, as people become more aware of it and see the hope, they can then transform the world with the help of micro-democracy. By eliminating states, the most dangerous war machine, peacefully solving disputes, and constructively running the world, this curse will be lifted. Over time, human culture will offset suffering with happiness little by little, replace greed with temperance, and finally reach a beautiful new world.

Original residents and migrants are allies of micro-democracy as well. The communication technology and transportation facilities have made travel more convenient and affordable. The constant movement of people is more prevalent and becomes a new normal. The increasing scale of migration has brought widespread impacts on economics, culture, and politics. Despite many positive elements in it, those adverse effects are more noticeable.[6,7] The core issue lies in the distribution of power and benefits between new immigrants and original residents—specifically, the oversimplification of immigrants' rights. In modern nations, when immigrants naturalize into citizens, they usually immediately entitle the same political rights as the original citizens. When there is an influx of a large number of immigrants in a short period of time, it forms a considerable political force capable of strongly impacting the local social order and lifestyle. If these immigrants share similar economic and cultural backgrounds, they are very likely to raise highly consistent political appeals and outnumber the votes of the originals. Such an impact on the original society will be more immediate and evident. As such, not only are they disrupted in daily lives, the original citizens may even become the minority in some contexts and lose their say of local affairs. Besides, immigrant groups sometimes bring larger families and often have a higher birth rate, so their proportion of the population will grow faster, which exacerbates the original citizens' anxiety and panic. Objectively speaking, their concern is not unreasonable. More and more examples have shown that the naturalization of immigrants is not always a process of absorbing alien economics and culture into the local ones but is sometimes more of an invasion. When the foreign economy and culture are relatively backward and large in scale, this invasion may lead to destruction and degradation of civilization.

Traveling and resettling in the world of micro-democracy will be easier for the migrants, and less a disturbance to the original residents. The unique design of voting weights would alleviate the impact of foreign economics and culture, and at the same time, buffer the potential contradictions and conflicts between immigrants and original residents. Original residents can adjust the time-based voting weights rules to gain the priority in decisions. When weighing the time factor highly, immigrants will no longer be able to control the results of decisions merely by outnumbering the original residents, thus reducing the impact on the local economy and culture. This design seems to cause inequalities in democratic rights. However, since migrants' previous residence time will also bring them extra voting weight in their place of origin, their chances of gaining time-based voting weight will be equal, from a holistic view. Besides, as immigrants continue to live in this new region, they will gradually obtain more time-based voting weight in the same way the original residents did, until eventually they become original residents themselves. The parameters the original residents set for the time-based voting weight shows to what extent and attitude they welcome the arrival of immigrants in general. In conjunction with the other two types of voting weights—that is, interests-relevant voting weights and knowledge voting weights—the local people can further fine-tune the acceptance towards immigrants with different economic conditions and knowledge levels. In turn, this will motivate immigrants to proactively improve their knowledge level to gain greater decision-making power at a faster pace. Ultimately, this interaction accelerates the improvement of the overall knowledge level of society.

It should be noted that immigrants and original residents are relative to each other. Any immigrant who has lived in a place long enough will become an original resident relative to newcomers. This identity is only tied to time and has nothing to do with other factors such as birthplace, race, ethnicity, religion, and culture. Although immigrants may be disadvantaged in decision-making due to falling short of time-based voting weight, such decisions should not affect their institutional human rights. They still have sufficient material conditions and legal protection to live a decent life in the area. They need only respect the current lifestyle and culture of the original people. Most importantly, voting weight adjustments are only allowed to apply to the factors of interest, knowledge, and time. These factors are equal to anyone, and so are the opportunities to accumulate them.

With the mechanism mentioned above, the relationship between immigrants and original residents will become more harmonious. Today's immigration problems are, in many cases, results of tyranny, war, and natural disasters, and the restrictions on the flow of people worsen these problems, making immigrants more likely to arrive to specific areas in a short period. In the world of micro-democracy, without tyranny and war, people can flow freely, and the moderate movement of people will become normal and no longer appear as an explosive social crisis. The only exception will be the refugee wave caused by natural disasters. Even in this case, since the entire territory of the micro-democracy world will accept refugees unconditionally, the burden will balance out across the whole world rather than putting all the pressure on limited areas.

Idealists and dreamers are also staunch allies of micro-democracy. They are receptive to fresh ideas and are willing to create new things. Idealism also fills them with courage, so they stand firm in trying to overcome obstacles in the most challenging moments and see defeating difficulties as proof of their self-value. They believe in the progress of society and desire to make the world a better place. However, in reality, few options were sufficiently practical and impactful. Unable to find something noble and worth fighting for, these warriors of the future are either lost in today's mediocre daily life or wasting out their passion and talent in those commercial games. Once they understand and agree with the idea of micro-democracy and realize that this is the key to fix all the problems, they will then devote themselves to a higher mission and become the pioneers and guides of this great cause and ignite hope in people around them.

Of course, the younger generation is also an ally of micro-democracy. Before the young hearts have been suffocated by heavy history and constrained by the shackles of life, they still have a magical power to create the possible from the impossible—the reality from the unrealistic—and use courage, passion, and the sincerity of life to build a heaven in the barren wilderness.

At last, any ordinary person, still young or not, still hoping for miracles or not, still believing great changes can occur in this world or not, as long as he or she holds the faith in freedom, equality, and justice, as long as he or she is furious at ugliness and longs for virtue, he or she is an ally of micro-democracy.

After recognizing the allies of micro-democracy, let us also point out some tough enemies:

Old politicians are enemies of micro-democracy. The "old" politicians refer to politicians, political parties, lobbyists, and government officials of almost all political systems who holds the decision-making power. Under the micro-democracy system, there are "new" politicians different from the former, including leaders, policonsultation agencies and political parties, and some government professionals with decision-making power at the microscopic level for routine executions.

Power is addicted to power. Old politicians' top priority is either to keep the power they already hold or to take the power others are holding. Sometimes they may also do some good deeds to serve the people, but that is more of a way and a byproduct of gaining and maintaining power. If necessary, they do not mind doing the cruelest evil for the same purpose. The hunger for power is a wild magnification of the desire for control and possessiveness that humans inherited from primitive organisms, which originated from the wisdom of survival in the harsh natural environment. However, human beings have sufficiently mastered science to free people from this endless crisis, and human culture is also ready to leap beyond biological and material needs to pursue spiritual abundance. To complete this leap, human civilization must transcend and eliminate this addiction to power, jumping out of eternal suffering and the fate of self-destruction. The evolution of political architecture is the process of restraining and domesticating power. People have invented some political systems, trying to guide the power to do more merit than evil through mutual restraint and supervision on the powerful, which unfortunately all fails. The fundamental flaw of the check and balance mechanism is that for the people in power, collusion is always an irresistible temptation, and the exchange of interests behind the scenes is far more profitable and safer than playing by the rules. Another common situation is that the powerful figures within the checks and balances are actually puppets manipulated by the same forces behind the scenes; the whole checks and balances system itself is a hoax.

Dictators are a special kind of old politician. Absolute power gives them overwhelming advantages so that they are concerned less about maintaining power, which give them energy to pursue grand achievement for self-fulfillment. If some of them have a wiser mind, these accomplishments are sometimes indeed beneficial to the people.

However, this is never assured. Those oppressed can only bend their knees to pray for a dictator's kindness and then are blessed with the little alms. Regrettably, absolute power is more inclined to seduce dictators into making arrogant acts, maybe only so can they enjoy the thrill of exercising power. Especially when their power is under threat, cold blood and brutality are almost always their first reaction, regardless of the cost to "their" people. Obviously, in the higher stages of civilization, the awakened people should hold their destiny in their own hands rather than betting on luck or begging for mercy.

The only antidote to the above maladies is the decomposition of centralized authorities, all the way back to the source of power. That is, every citizen deciding on every issue is the only way to provide the ultimate solution to this problem. Micro-democracy does exactly this. New politicians in micro-democracy do not really possess power as citizens can revoke the voting delegations at any time to retrieve control. It is pointless to build a mansion of power on quicksand, so new politicians will turn back and focus on serving their people faithfully instead of chasing power.

When the micro-democracy world reclaims the power and returns it to the public, the old politicians will not surrender easily. They will sabotage the technology to fail the micro-democracy system or provoke chaos. They will attack or bribe leaders and followers of micro-democracy to make them give up their ideals. They will pretend to compromise and deceive the people into staying in the status quo with pretty bait. They will divide people by alienating race, nation, religion, and class to make them misunderstand, hate, and fight with each other, rendering them unable to cooperate. They will use the fear of the unknown to overwhelm the people, and all measures possible to prevent the arrival of the new world. The road of micro-democracy will indeed be bumpy, but as long as people anticipate these obstacles in advance and see through the enemies' tactics—as long as people realize that the superiority of micro-democracy could never be provided and replaced by the old world—they will then persevere until the final victory. The only thing to be vigilant about is not to compromise. Never place a seat for an old politician in a temple of the new world. If they genuinely change their minds, then they shall grow into new politicians, rediscovering their value in the world of micro-democracy.

Additionally, nationalists are the enemies of micro-democracy. They are lovers of the nation and country of their own, but also fearers and haters of the others. Just like the tribal loyalists in the primitive society, the family loyalists in the feudal society, the loyalists of nations and countries are also a product of times. People tend to favor things they are familiar with and which are controllable, but they are fearful and hostile to unknowns. This fear and hostility tend to make unfamiliar groups conflict rather than cooperate. In their eyes, "our people" are real human beings, while the outside world is full of homogeneous fuzzy symbols. Those outsiders are not living beings, but devils with feuds. Under the shadow of this thinking, people will resist migration freedom, refuse to cooperate, and reject the coming of micro-democracy.

Actually, if nationalists get the chance to mix with the peoples of other nations and countries and know each other more deeply in person, they will likely replace national stereotypes with thoughts, characters, preferences, and behaviors of each individual. It will promote them from loyalists of nations to lovers of humanity and the world. However, nationalists and patriots are also the old politicians' target for recruitment. The old politicians will keep reminding them of the glory and humiliation in history, use the honor and hatred of the collectives to reinforce their identity, obliterate their individuality and humanity, and eventually shape them into warriors of the old world. After all, self-negating is hard and painful, but at the same time, waking and growing are joyful and refreshing. The micro-democracy should make best efforts on winning over nationalists' hearts with rationality, open mindedness, and love for humanity, so that they will self-transcend and stand with progress and the future.

Moreover, the *New World Order*[8] is an enemy of micro-democracy. The new world order mentioned here is not any emerging order for worldwide operations. It specifically refers to the alliance of global capitalist forces with secret religious groups, and the organizations built to achieve their hidden agenda. On the surface, they also attempt to establish a centralized world government lead by the elites, but their true core circle is very low-key and extremely secretive. This cover-up and mystery enhance their strength and help them perform outlaw operations quietly. Money and Christianity are their primary instruments, so their infiltration into the political organizations and power institutions of the Western democracies is also the deepest and most successful. However, they are by no means lovers of democracy and human rights. They never hesitate to use conspiracy, lies, corruption, dictators, and wars to achieve the purpose of exercising power and control, at the cost of the lives of innocent civilians by millions. In essence, the new world order is a modern slavery society run by invisible hands, under the cloak of globalization.

The idea of abolishing national borders and establishing a world government may confuse people to believe that the new world order and micro-democracy share some commonalities. On the contrary, this makes them two enemies. This is because their global centralized government will integrate the evil forces into their most potent and deceptive form, causing the most severe threat and damage to the micro-democracy. Therefore, builders of micro-democracy must clearly recognize the fundamental distinctions between new world order and micro-democracy: First of all, a micro-democracy government is decentralized and completely distributed. It is a system of direct democracy and will never adopt a representative system. Second, the micro-democracy government must disclose all the information fully, from collecting to processing. It prevents any misinformation and disinformation from being used to manipulate public opinion. Finally, and most importantly, in combating the new world order and other enemies, there must be a reliable mechanism to restore the micro-democracy system automatically and quickly from any temporary deviation caused by war or natural disasters. In particular, this mechanism must be able to detect and address cases of passively handling or deliberately prolonging external threats, so that the new world order will find no room under the shell of micro-democracy to parasitize and steal the fruits of democracy.

To undermine people's support for micro-democracy, the enemies will undoubtedly slander it, causing misunderstanding, fear, and hostility against it. Therefore, it is necessary to make preventive clarifications and explanations of some of the slights and questions that micro-democracy is most likely to face.

Numerous sci-fi films, TV shows, and books have painted scenes of artificial intelligence gone out of control, where tangible or invisible robot rule, enslave, and even slaughter humans. It's imaginable that the threat of artificial intelligence is an easy argument against micro-democracy. Since micro-democracy countries run all the decision-making processes on information systems, is there a risk the system will be hijacked by the machines and become a tool for ruling humans? As an expert of information technology, I would like to provide some simple explanations for dispelling readers' doubts.

Many people are convinced that the future will look as vivid as the computer-generated imagery in films, and many companies are also trying to excite people with stories of artificial intelligence as a commercial gimmick. Still, in the eyes of serious technical experts, artificial intelligence technology is considerably far away from being able to grant machines real self-consciousness. Although many products with impressive linguistic and behavioral interaction capabilities have appeared on the market, they are only simulating human behaviors without truly comprehending, reasoning, or thinking. In the field of information science, the simulations of thinking processes are implemented as algorithms, which are computer programs written by programmers. However, many of the core mechanisms of human brain functions, such as association, self-consciousness, and the subconscious, have not yet been thoroughly understood, let alone imitated and replicated. Therefore, all such algorithms today can barely simulate the most superficial and simple parts of human thinking. In the final analysis, the developers' own (human) capabilities are the ultimate constraints to any algorithm. At present, computer scientists have not found any method to enable machines to develop new algorithms on their own. Until a breakthrough happens in this domain, the computer will never surpass the thinking ability of humans.

Compared to the human brain, computers indeed outperform us in certain aspects like data processing, storage, and retrieval. By developing these advantages to the extreme and adding some fancy anthropomorphic features, computers can sometimes show unexpected stunning effects, leaving people with the impression that machines surpass humans. Of course, technology companies are also happy to render a fancy vision of artificial intelligence to please customers and shareholders. But behind these illusions, the machines are still only tools operated by humans, without self-consciousness, without souls, and without self-evolution capability.

Whether the machine can eventually produce self-consciousness is still controversial. At least there is still no convincing and reliable evidence or signs that the technology is approaching such a breakthrough. Humans may never be able to give machines a truly independent reasoning capability and soul. However, I am still cautiously optimistic that perhaps after a long and unremitting endeavor, people will finally acquire adequate technology to enable machines to gain self-awareness and other life features. But even if this happens, it will not affect micro-democracy information systems.

This is because any program that can, if ever possible, make the machine self-aware and truly intelligent must emerge from a set of complex, specialized algorithms, called algorithm-intensive programs. Micro-democracy information systems do not need to and should not be using an algorithm-intensive program. Though the amount of data processed by the micro-democracy information system is massive, the processing logic for these data is relatively simple as most of it is pure numerical calculations and statistics, with a complexity comparable to that of today's core banking systems. It falls into the category of the data-intensive system of records, an entirely different species from algorithm-intensive programs.

All the micro-democracy core logic is entirely in this book. Any citizen with an elementary education should be able to understand it effortlessly. Correspondingly, the micro-democracy information system implements it with fairly straightforward algorithms. Most software developers who have received comprehensive programming training should be able to build them without hassle. The complete program source code of this system must be unconditionally published so that anybody can learn and inspect its internal logic to safeguard it from malicious code. On the premise of achieving its functional goals, its architecture and design should be as simple as possible. A system built with straightforward algorithms as such will never produce so-called self-consciousness. Public supervision also blocks any attempt to introduce suspiciously complex algorithms into the system.

As an extra note, in micro-democracy systems, the vast majority of decisions come from statistics of people's voting records, indicating that people are the ones who make decisions, whereas machines merely assist calculations. The only exceptions are the decisions of judicial cases. The micro-democracy system may introduce automated decision-making, so that massive historical legal precedents can be efficiently retrieved and referenced, making the legal decisions fairer and more consistent. However, even in this case, the machine-assisted decision can never be the final one. Whenever any party appeals, the final decision must be made by the human. Therefore, micro-democracy decision-making power is always entirely in the hands of people, not machines.

Another threat often portrayed in literary and artistic works is the omnipresent surveillance, control, enslavement, and persecution of the public by dictators, police states, or hackers with the help of electronic devices and networks. Facing the overwhelming advantages of high-tech tools, people helplessly surrender their human rights and societal freedom. Such a scene is no longer science fiction but is rapidly becoming a reality. If there is any technology that can help rulers to consolidate and expand their power, to control the public, they will put it into use and exert its maximum outcome without hesitation. By plotting security incidents and exaggerating the threats, they widely deploy such technologies in the name of national security and social order. Also, some improvements in the efficiency of public services and the convenience of life helps to convince the public to adopt these technologies. Without knowing it, the rulers have built vast surveillance networks to spy on citizens' lives with millions of cameras, to control people's entire finances with electronic money, and to screen citizens' communication with social media, and brainwash them with misinformation. Like so, the rulers can act as the shepherd herding the flock, playing god, harvesting the skin, wool, and meat as they wish. When people realize what is happening if they ever do, everything has already become irreparable.

So, will the micro-democracy information system, which is also a large-scale network system, become a tool to fuel the above threats or even serve as the core of these conspiracies? The answer is no, for the following reasons:

Firstly, micro-democracy is non-mandatory. Citizens are free to decide the extent to which they like to use the system and participate in democratic decision-making. If an individual wishes to be involved deeply in politics, he or she may need to provide more personal information to receive additional voting weights or to qualify for certain roles like public opinion agents. But, if he or she prefers to completely separate from political activities, he or she can ignore it entirely. For such a case, in the micro-democracy system, this individual's voting weights will be exercised by his or her designated delegates or the default primary party.

Secondly, under the micro-democracy system, information is absolutely open and equally accessible to everybody. The complete life cycle of any resolution is under the spotlight and microscope throughout the procedure defined with open rules, and these rules and procedures themselves are configured by all people democratically as well. Citizens have the choice of whether their voting records are public or not, but the voting records of other policonsultation agencies should be completely open to the public. The right to know, under the institutional human rights, requires that any public information should be made available to the general public without discrimination or condition. It includes but is not limited to any social information related to the voting weights, all information about public events, and surveillance in public places. At the same time, privacy of individuals is strictly protected, no system has the right to record and disclose the private information without the consent of the person. Under the above principles, there is no more privileged minority that can spy on private lives, obtain and block exclusive information under the pretext of government secrecy, nor filter and twist public information, and block citizens' speech.

Further, the micro-democracy information system is independent. It needs not and should not bind with any external control system (such as surveillance systems, public facility control systems, non-institutional human rights social services and business systems, etc.), and certainly not depend on them. Therefore, the risk of exploiting the vulnerabilities of those connected systems to control and sabotage is next to none.

Not only will the micro-democracy system refrain from becoming the dictator's accomplice to rule over the people, but it will actually accomplish the opposite by defeating it. As nowadays governments are accelerating the deployment of technology for monitoring, controlling, and enslaving, more and more people see through it. However, while people show strong resistance against technology, they target the crux of the issue less: the ruling class and the political system itself. Being off target, such anti-technology resistances not only don't fix any problem but are easily vilified as extremists or even terrorist acts and therefore marginalized, hindering the development of widespread support of the masses. Micro-democracy addresses the problems from a deeper level. It reveals the logical relationship between technology and policies, identifies which exact technologies and policies impose threats on the public's well-being and free society. Then, it constructively proposes the ways and principles of using advanced technology to benefit humanity. In the final analysis, the use of information is not what people should oppose; the asymmetry of information is. If all people can access information on an equal and complete basis, then the information will become people's best friend.

The micro-democracy system has many adjustable parameters, including voting weight formulas, delegated votes remuneration formulas, default delegation selection rules, resolution re-validation rules, qualifications of public opinion agents, and decision-making processes, etc. Different settings of these parameters will result in different decision-making styles. The dynamic of parameter combinations, coupled with the historical resolutions and ever-changing external conditions, will make the evolution of a micro-democracy society full of possibilities and variations. The study of these combinations and dynamics is enough to form independent disciplines of politics and public administration. The regularity will be more predictable and controllable as people's experience accumulates, helping them to discover a favorable balance between stability and development of the society. At the beginning of micro-democracy practices, people will inevitably go through a curve of learning and a journey of trial and error. At this stage, some unreasonable configurations will likely appear, causing some temporary defects and confusion. The dynamic adjustment and peaceful competition among regions will help those more scientific and superior configurations emerge, gradually washing out those that are most unreasonable, thereby fine-tuning the micro-democracy world. However, the initial chaos may still be unavoidable, as enemies of micro-democracy will not miss out an opportunity to attack the micro-democracy system during the temporary difficulties of its early stage.

Although the initial experimental period of micro-democracy is unavoidable, some strategies can help to reduce the adverse effects. The first important factor is to avoid overly aggressive parameter configuration. Even if people want to make some bold attempts, they should break it down into stages so that each step is relatively small and easy to adjust. Secondly, they should avoid frequent iterations and allow enough time for each configuration to play out and fully reveal its characteristics, so as to guide subsequent adjustments to be more reasonable and scientific. Also, it is important to divide the decision-making regions finer, even if it tends to be too much at first. In this way, people can experiment with different configurations in various regions in parallel, compare their advantages and disadvantages, and observe their interactions, so that the science of micro-democracy configuration evolves faster. Also, this approach makes it relatively easy to isolate some suboptimal settings so that their adverse effects are restrained and reduced. Finally, the people should set reasonable expectations of the perfecting process of micro-democracy and consciously adopt a relatively conservative strategy so that they will be better prepared for difficulties in the early trial and error process. In this way, the slander, threats, and destruction in the early days may be mitigated, so that micro-democracy can enter a state of stable operation more quickly and smoothly.

Personal attacks have always been a repertory for politics, particularly in the representative democracy, and the reason is apparent: The identity of the representative comes from the vote which depends on the candidate's public image. To undermine the reputation of the competitor is to weaken his or her strength and magnify ones' own advantage. Moreover, personal attacks are also a trick of diverting attention—so that people's focus is drawn to candidates' traits rather than those public affairs decisions that really matter.

Enemies will undeniably use their familiar weapons to assault the builders, advocates, and participants of micro-democracy, launch personal attacks against them, question their motives, denigrate their personalities, and exclude people with certain identities and backgrounds. However, these attacks are much less lethal to micro-democracy. This is because acquiring voters' voting power is not the goal of micro-democracy activists, and they will not be granted any privileges from the political system. Even if they receive voters' delegation, the voters can withdraw it at any time. Therefore, the political figures' motives, personal conduct, and abilities do not really affect the rights and interests of the people. When people realize this fact, they will move their eyes to the advantages of the system itself and the content of each specific issue, rather than the personal problems of the new politicians. In the end, it will backfire on the old politicians who play the personal attack game.

When the entire country runs on an information system, its reliability and safety are vital. Security incidents happen all the time in the age of the internet, and concerns over it are totally reasonable. Of course, the enemies will never miss such a chance to exaggerate potential risks of the micro-democracy system, question its feasibility, and undermine people's confidence.

For those common security threats to information systems, industries have developed very mature technologies and comprehensive strategies to prevent and respond. In fact, almost all safety accidents can be attributed to insufficient investment, poor design and implementation, and imperfect safety regulations. They can be avoided through sound defensive measures, or their impact can be mitigated to an acceptable level through appropriate contingency strategies. For example, in dealing with the situation of equipment failure, tactics like redundancy, load balancing, and failover can avoid single-point failures to prevent service interruptions. For the threat of computer virus and hacking, choosing a reliable operating system with robust security protection can significantly reduce the risk, even more so for a strictly partitioned network environment. For example, with these stringent protections, IBM's mainframe core system[9], widely used in the financial sector, has never been successfully penetrated or infected by any virus for decades. Apart from the strategy of building an indestructible central fortress, with the development of cloud computing technologies, distributed and decentralized security strategies have also emerged.[10] In such architecture, there are instances of the services being hosted at many nodes across the entire network, collaborating with and backing up each other. When accidents occur, causing some nodes to fail, other normal nodes are still sufficient to service the overall uninterrupted operation of the platform and also to assist the failed nodes to recover.

The records of protecting the critical information systems show that the defenders presented an overwhelming success over the attackers and intruders. Even for those rare failure incidents, the systems can always be repaired and restored within a short time. Among those accidents, the majority are characterized by leaking and theft of confidential information; it is much rarer to tamper with data or destroy the system itself. The micro-democracy idea believes that political activities should be open and transparent to all citizens, so its data is not supposed to be confidential in the first place. On the contrary, the system should actively provide channels and functions to make the information accessible to the public as much as possible. There is no such thing as a "theft" of information since it belongs to everybody. The only exception is a small amount of personal information of citizens stored in the system for assisting operations, like for calculating voting weights or delegating. This kind of information only involves the citizens' identity information and records of their political activities, that do not necessarily contain sensitive personal life information.

Another typical attack is maliciously consuming massive system resources, making the system inaccessible to the users for a certain period of time. This type of attack is commonly known as the Denial-of-Service (DoS) attack[11], often causing major financial losses for large-scale commercial operations. After all, every minute the system goes offline may result in the loss of customers and diversion of sales to competitors. However, for micro-democracy operations, such an incident has a relatively mild impact. This is because the time-sensitivity for voting activities is low, and therefore postponing for hours or even days will not have a big impact from the perspective of political activity in most cases. Of course, in theory, a micro-democracy system should be able to provide uninterrupted services throughout the day. Still, if compared with the five-day, eight-hour working routines of current political institutions and governments, it has far exceeded the basic requirement for government operation. Even if the system service level downgrades a lot, for example, providing only 12 hours of service per day, giving the rest of the time all for system maintenance, or allowing frequent outage, although less pleasant, it is still actually sufficient to support the political operations.

No matter how strict security measures are, a recovery plan is always necessary. Today, there are many sophisticated and reliable technical solutions for system protection and disaster recovery, which are still evolving and developing. The introduction of such solutions is obviously beyond the scope of this book, but this knowledge is widely available from various channels for interested readers to study further.

Beyond those conventional technical solutions, one unique approach will provide unparalleled protection for micro-democracy. That is to regularly distribute all system source code and all democratic operation data to the personal devices of all citizens. Based on the estimation of the possible data volume, if only text and numerical data are backed up, with the appropriate data compression technology, the data package will be far smaller than the video files of a movie. Any current high-end smartphone is sufficient to save this data effortlessly. In a high-speed network environment, the transmission of the entire data can be completed within minutes or sooner. In this way, the complete knowledge and historical data of micro-democracy will reside in every electronic device, just like there's a copy of genes in each cell of every living creature. With this protection, no matter what kind of damage the micro-democracy system suffers, as long as one such electronic device survives in the whole world, the function of the micro-democracy system and its entire history can be completely restored.

From the above analysis, technology will not be an obstacle to the realization of micro-democracy; rather, those powerful human enemies are the real threat. Taking this into consideration, let's picture the three most likely implementation paths to the birth of the micro-democracy countries:

*Path One: **Airborne***

Pilot the micro-democracy in a special administrative region, gradually improve and expand until a state takes shape, or directly convert some independent mini countries into micro-democracy nations by directly restructuring the government and enforcing micro-democracy laws.

This path requires the cooperation of local residents, the support of visionary politicians, and considerable financial aid to establish and improve the micro-democracy infrastructure. In an ideal situation, it is the simplest and most reasonable way to realize micro-democracy. The entire process operates in a prepared and orderly manner with thoughtful planning and sufficient material supplies, so that the life transition of local people will be stable and smooth. However, some prerequisites needed for this path are hard to meet. Since micro-democracy is the transcendence and negation of modern nations, and old politicians are its natural enemies, delimiting special zones in an existing modern nation with the support of old politicians may only be possible in some extreme cases. For example, political and economic crises may force politicians to compromise with public opinions. However, in such critical situations, the lack of resources and social instability also makes the implementation more complicated. Funding support is crucial, but such funding support should remain unconditional and selfless, without trading any special privilege with anyone, to avoid micro-democracy being hijacked and manipulated by capital. Another risk is that the enemies fake their support and secretly carry out interference and destruction. What they really want is to show the world a catastrophic failure and dispel people's trust and hope for the micro-democracy revolution. The pioneers of micro-democracy must be wise to see through the types and true intentions of various supporters, reject and resist false and malicious ones, adhere to the principles of micro-democracy, not make seemingly harmless but practically dangerous compromises.

Path Two: **Rebuild**

Create a brand-new micro-democracy country from scratch in a fresh, uninhabited continent and rebuild the civilization directly.

Because modern nations have long occupied all the fertile land on this planet, what is left is barren deserts, wilderness, ice fields, and oceans. It requires like-minded pioneers, with unyielding conviction and sacrifice, to move human civilization to primitive land with extraordinary courage and resilience. No doubt, this path faces enormous challenges in terms of space, time, material, and technology. However, this approach has eased the difficulty of transforming existing residents' ideas and lifestyles. Since all participants are champions of micro-democracy, the achievement and implementation of resolutions will be more efficient and effective, while also making the disruption of external enemies easier to detect and handle. For these enthusiastic and optimistic pioneers, accepting the anticipated difficulties and overcoming them together, creating the epic achievements of the new civilization will not be a pain, but the source of heroic motivation and happiness.

Path Three: **Transform**

Encourage people to practice micro-democracy in various environments and conditions. Start with daily life decisions, instead of the pursuit of using it directly for government operation and policymaking all at once. After people become familiar with it, and the techniques of micro-democracy configuration become polished and mature, this decision-making method will naturally extend to more complex public affairs until it is capable of simulating government in the virtual network world.

Of course, the simplification of micro-democracy in early practice will cripple many core characteristics and advantages; the absence of institutional human rights will especially affect the overall equality of decision-making. When people are getting aware of this problem, they will be increasingly eager to implement these institutional human rights in the real world, forming a strong drive for people to bring micro-democracy to the political life of reality. If the simplified micro-democracy operates in a cross-border virtual world, then when it comes to the real world, it is likely to be cross-border as well or even of the global scope. For example, multiple existing countries may gradually surrender some decision-making authority to the micro-democracy system in the virtual world following strong demands of people. After one slice of power is transferred and becomes stable, other pieces may follow. If such path works, the impact on people will be minimal, as will the risk of the realization of micro-democracy.

However, this path has its particular risks: The entire process may be hijacked by old politicians. Globalization elites of the old world may take advantage of the situation that institutional human rights are absent in the simplified micro-democracy and abuse the extra voting weights from their existing knowledge and experience so that they can consolidate and strengthen their privileges during the transition, then continue to enjoy those benefits of the old world for a very long time. Or even worse, they might slyly transform the micro-democracy system into a different system to privilege them. In response to this problem, special arrangements are necessary for the transition period. That is, there needs to be a shortening of the active time of the resolutions made before the presence of institutional human rights, and a re-validation of all policies as soon as the institutional human rights are implemented. In other words, all decisions made in simplified micro-democracy mode are considered temporary, with only the re-validation under the presence of institutional human rights qualifying them as official resolutions.

None of the above paths rely on violence or destruction. Without a doubt, people have every right to resist, even violently, the oppression and persecution of the old system, as this is undoubtedly morally justifiable. However, rebellious violence and oppressive violence are equally dangerous and toxic to micro-democracy, and they can easily deviate the revolutionary cause from its original intention and let force seize the throne of power. Therefore, the non-violent path is the preferred choice for micro-democracy over others. Even if in achieving micro-democracy, some violence against the old forces must be a necessary evil, then upon succeeding, additional de-violent steps should then be exercised for purification and normalization of the system.

 # Science

The operation of micro-democracy is implemented with rules and parameters. Under the micro-democracy system, a specific combination of rules and parameters is a set of technical settings. Individual regions at all levels may run with its independent technical settings. Each set of settings has its unique characteristics, which has a meaningful influence on the decision-making style, lifestyle, and social development direction of that region. The inter-regional interplay and societal self-evolution essentially reflect the interactions of their underlying technical settings. It forms an ecosystem when all the regions constantly interact with each other within a micro-democracy country. The study of these rules, parameters, combinations, and their social implications is a science in its nature. This science gives people a new instrument for understanding and predicting the effects of the above elements on a micro-democracy society and responding consciously to align with the goal of maximizing social utility.

Micro-democracy encourages the diversity and free development of society, so it is open and inclusive for different technical settings. It promotes the full development and evolution of societies in different regions, providing broader choices for the directions of civilization. However, it is also necessary to be aware that certain extreme values or particular combinations harm equality, freedom, and social utility and thus require extra caution.

For example, in setting the weight ratio, if the interests relevant voting weight is disproportionately higher than other weights, and the personal asset is the main element of the formula, then the capital and wealth, rather than people, actually gain significant political power. It will bring enormous benefits to the few rich. And if the proportion of time-relevant voting weight increases exponentially, the elderly and original residents obtain the overwhelming advantage of civil rights, making the young people and immigrants severely suppressed. For another example, if in democratic procedures the resolutions re-validation frequency is too low, such as per fifty years or more, or the triggering conditions are too harsh, it will void the re-validation mechanism. As such, the vested interests can lock the resolution in their favor for a long time or even forever. Clearly, the importance of the micro-democracy principles is self-evident, yet only in cooperation with reasonable technical settings can the expected goal be achieved.

Fortunately, the micro-democracy institutional human rights provide an ultimate safeguard, even when extreme settings and unusual combinations of those parameters appear; people are still protected and have the effective channel to correct these deviations. Institutional human rights are virtually mandatory restrictions of political parameters, preventing them from reaching specific extreme ranges. In this sense, micro-democracy is nothing but a political system that uniquely presets its institutional human rights parameters. Beyond these parameter restrictions, other political systems can also be parametrically defined, represented, and categorized.

In order to study the nature of political systems under the surface, the remaining part of this chapter introduces a new analytical model of social democracy along with some quantitative indicators. With these tools people can conduct objective qualitative analysis and horizontal comparison of various political systems, and reasonably conclude the superiority of micro-democracy. However, for readers who are not familiar with scientific analytical methods, the following content may appear obscure. In such a case, skipping this part won't affect the reader's to fully grasping the concepts of micro-democracy theory.

Political Decision-making Granularity Analysis (PDGA) studies the granular distribution and combination of subjects and objects in political decision-making. The purpose is to find its decision-making characteristics, patterns, and then predict its impact on decision results (abbreviated as *Granular Analysis* or *GA*). It mainly involves the following indicators and concepts:

- *Political Decision-making Subject Granularity (PDSG)* refers to the proportion of decision-making subjects (those who participate in political decision-making and have a substantial impact on its outcome) compared to the population (abbreviated as *Subject Granularity* or *SG*). Its values range from 0 to 1 (or 0% to 100%). Value 0 indicates that the subject mentioned above is the smallest decision-making unit in the society—that is, individual citizens— which reflects that the ratio of an individual to the total number of citizens is approximately 0%. A gradual increase of this value indicates that the population representation proportion of the subject of the decision-making—that is, the representatives or the delegates—increased gradually in the context of decision-making activities. Value 1 represents the highest and sole decision-making representative or delegate, that is, a dictator, who has the highest power in the nation and makes decisions for all citizens (100%).

- *Political Decision-making Object Granularity (PDOG)* refers to the proportion of citizens covered and affected by the decision-making objects (that is, issues of political decision-making) in the decision-making activities (abbreviated as *Object Granularity* or *OG*). Its value ranges from 0 to 1 (or 0% to 100%). Value 0 means extreme fine-grained decision-making, the scope of which is limited to a specific individual or a tiny group, whose number accounts for approximately 0% of the population. A gradual increase of this value indicates the object of the decision, the decision issue, affecting a gradually increasing proportion of the population. Value 1 means major universal issues, such as national policies, etc. that all citizens (100% of the population) will be affected by.

- *Political Decision-making Granularity Map (PDGM)* is a two-dimensional chart with subject and object granularities as the vertical and horizontal axes, respectively, to reveal the decision-making mode of the government (abbreviated as *Granularity Map* or *GM*). Figure 9.1 is an example of a granularity map showing the decision model for a fictional political system. The gray shaded area in this example is the *Political Decision-making Granularity Pattern (PDGP)* of this political system, which helps analyze the pattern and characteristics of its decision-making (abbreviated as *Granularity Pattern* or *GP*). Generally speaking, the smaller the vertical axis value is, the more involved individual citizens or small groups will be in political decision-making. It indicates that the political activities are closer to populism and popularized for the corresponding granularity range. A larger value shows that the political decision of the corresponding scope of object granularity is more concentrated to fewer decision-makers. To some extent, an increase in this value also reflects the improvement of the efficiency of political decision-making. However, decision-making efficiency is not necessarily proportional to the quality of the decisions. This is because there are different perspectives and criteria for measuring the quality of decisions, and there are varied interpretations. The most common situation is that decision-makers make the most favorable decisions for their own class and group, and other people and groups bear the corresponding costs and adverse effects. Therefore, the judges' positions determine the conclusions. If we choose to judge from the perspective of social utilitarianism, we can roughly infer that the smaller the value of the vertical axis— that is, the more the decision is made by the general public directly—the higher the social utility is likely to be and the society is more in line with the goal pursued by micro-democracy.

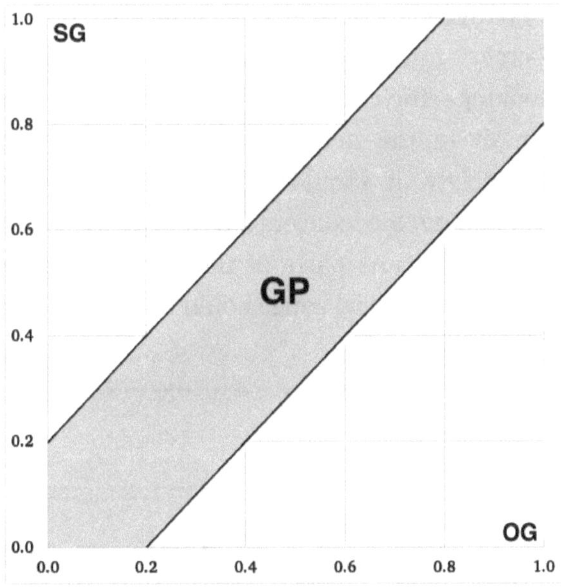

Figure 9.1 Granularity map: a fictional political system.

- *Political Decision-making Granularity Characteristic Zone (PDGCZ)* refers to the five areas lying in the granularity map that represent different decision-making styles and characteristics (abbreviated as *Granularity Characteristic Zone* or *GCZ*). As shown in Figure 9.2, the five areas framed by dotted lines and indicated by numbers are Zone 1 (*Dictatorial Zone*), Zone 2 (*Concentrated Zone*), Zone 3 (*Neutral Zone*), Zone 4 (*Collaborative Zone*), and Zone 5 (*Democratic Zone*). As the name implies, the zones that the granularity pattern fall into indicate the decision-making style adopted by the society for the issues of the corresponding object granularity. For example, as shown in the chart, the fictional political system takes an autocratic decision-making approach on the overall decision-making issues (zone 1), and a micro decision-making approach on

169

the democratic decision-making approach (zone 5). The transition of decision-making styles for issues in between is roughly even. Judging from the view of micro-democracy, the granularity pattern of a purely democratic system should reside in the democracy zone completely. But if balancing with the decision-making efficiency factor, an ideal granularity pattern may better sit in the neutral and collaborative zones. For a democratic society, it should be vigilant when the granularity pattern extends to the concentration and dictatorial zones. A scenario in which some parts of the granularity pattern to fall entirely into the dictatorial zone should be absolutely avoided.

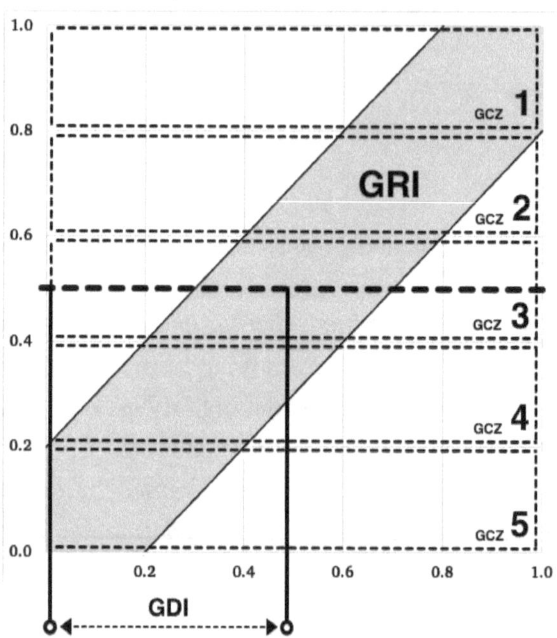

Figure 9.2 Granularity map: a fictional political system, overlaid with granularity characteristic zones

- *Political Decision-making Granularity Resiliency Index (PDGRI)* shows how flexibly a political system can adjust its decision-making style (abbreviated as *Granularity Resiliency Index* or

GRI). In the granularity map, it is the area of the granularity pattern—that is, the area of the shadow—ranging from 0 to 1. This value measures how much room the society has in terms of choices of decision-making methods. For example, based on simple geometric calculations, the granularity resiliency index of the fictional political system shown in Figure 9.1 is approximately 0.36. Presumably, the political system with a smaller granularity resiliency index is more consistent or stable, and those with a higher value has a larger room for changes.

- *Political Decision-making Granularity Democracy Index (PDGDI)* indicates the degree of a political system's leaning towards choosing decision-making methods in favor of democracy (abbreviated as *Granularity Democracy Index* or *GDI*). As shown in Figure 9.2, a horizontal dashed line divides the intensity chart into the upper half (*Authoritarian Domain*) and the lower half (*Democracy Domain*) with the subject granularity 0.5 as the edge. In any longitudinal section, if the length of the granularity pattern falls into the democracy domain is longer than that of the authoritarian domain, then the projection of this section cast on the horizontal axis is counted into this index. The accumulated lengths of the above projection in the granularity map is the granularity democracy index of the political system. The value ranges from 0 to 1. A higher value indicates that the decisions generally tend to be made democratically in this system. For example, the granularity democracy index shown in Figure 9.1 is 0.50.

The above tools help people quantitatively analyze and compare a certain political system:

In the **Slavery** society, all decisions were made by the slave-owner class, which was a small minority of the population. The majority of the people, the slaves, had no say in decision-making at all, even for those very personal matters. Therefore, as shown in Figure 9.3, the slave society's granularity pattern is in the dictatorial zone entirely. Its granularity resiliency index is minimal (not higher than 0.05); thus, the system is very stable. Its granularity democracy index is 0, which indicates that there is no possibility for the main population (slaves and serfs) to enjoy democracy.

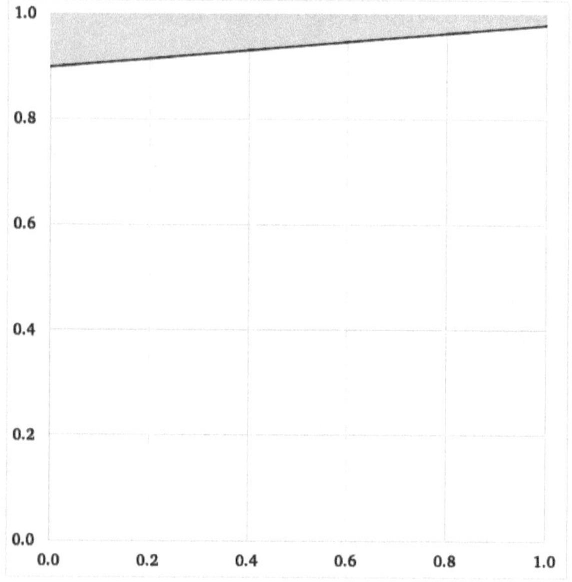

Figure 9.3 Granularity map: Slavery

The societies depicted in this granularity map include those ancient slavery societies such as Egypt, as well as many modern nations ruled by lords, nobles, and serf-owners. Perhaps their polity structures have many significant differences in form and etiquette from typical slavery, thus are often categorized as feudal or serfdom. However, from the perspective of granularity analysis, there is no essential difference in their modes of decision-making.

Anarchism opposes the governmental ruling itself. It advocates micro-autonomy and mutual assistance among people for resolving personal and public decisions. In turn, it weakens people's ability to collaborate in larger-scale activities, making policymaking in vast regions nearly impossible. As shown in Figure 9.4, for the scale of modern countries, anarchism can only partially cover the lower range of object granularity. Its granularity resiliency index is next to none (approximately 0.02) and, therefore, extremely stable in its applicable range. Its granularity democracy index (approximately 0.40) completely covers the limited scope of its object granularity. However, this kind of democracy merely embodies the decision-making power over citizens' personal affairs rather than public policies.

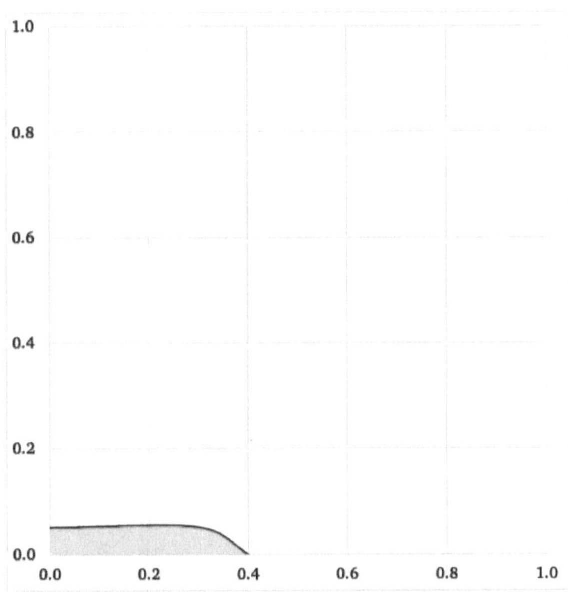

Figure 9.4 Granularity map: Anarchy

Autocracy, from the perspective of political decision-making, covers a variety of political systems, including most of the feudal system, the traditional monarchy, the fascist state system, and centralization systems denoted by various other names. Its core feature is the hierarchical organization of power, where the decision-making and action are based on the unconditional obey and execution of superior power's wills, rather than by the functional roles. Therefore, the upper decision-makers have absolute authority to overwrite the decisions made by the lower levels. Hence, the top authority (usually the sole dictator, or possibly a minimal number of court nobles, lords, or committee members) has the ultimate and final decision-making power on all public affairs. Compared with slavery, autocracy's granularity pattern extends to the lower range of subject granularity. This is because, in the autocracy society, more social members get some access to higher classes and participate in the lower-level decision-making. Complicated and huge bureaucratic decision-making systems were established, for the upper leaders to delegate decision-making power to the lower-level officials to share their burden.

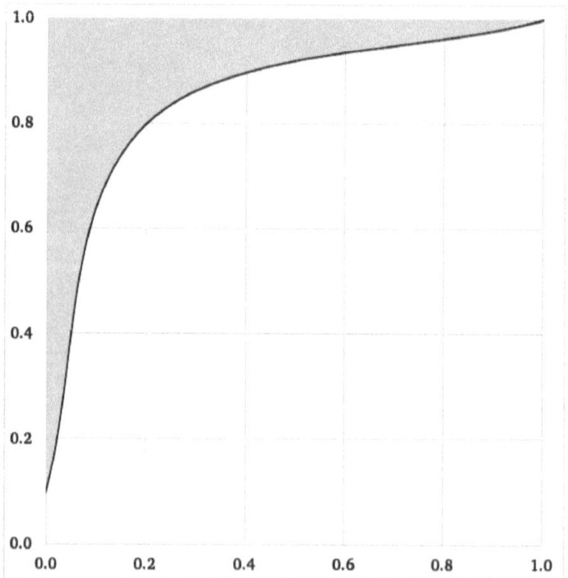

Figure 9.5 Granularity map: Autocracy

As shown in Figure 9.5, autocracy's granularity pattern covers the whole range of object granularity at the top edge, where the subject granularity value is 1, representing the sole dictator. With the object granularity dropping, the curve shows decision-makers at lower levels were allowed to decide on some finer-grained issues, as the bureaucratic structure sinks gradually. Autocracy's granularity resiliency index is about 0.20, and the contraction space of elasticity is towards the boundary; that is, the dictator makes more macro decisions personally. Its granularity democracy index is 0.

The granularity map of **Representative Democracy** is rather complicated because of its two unique features. First, representative democracy usually has a hierarchy of powers and separate checks and balances, so the highest leaders of the country do not have the power to make decisions on all public matters like the dictators of autocracy regimes do. As shown in the granularity map, at the top edge, the granularity pattern only covers the right part, instead of the entire top border, indicating that the top leaders of the country are more inclined to make macro-level decisions. It is usually the lower layer decision-making bodies and administrative agencies that decide on public affairs at the micro-level. The referendum is another feature, which makes it possible for all citizens to determine very few global public affairs under exceptional circumstances. As reflected in the granularity map, there is a thin vertical stripe at the far right where the object granularity value is 1. In Figure 9.6, the granularity pattern is surrounded by two solid lines, called the *Public Opinion Boundary* and the *Institutional Boundary* from left to right. The public opinion boundary is mainly backed by the power of public opinion, which prevents the regime from degenerating to the left and becoming an autocracy. The institutional boundary is a product of the inherent structure of the representative system, preventing the people from directly making decisions on public affairs. Additionally, there is a dashed line in between, which indicates the limit that the public opinion boundary can be pushed to the right. This actually reflects the political reality of today's world: Many regimes self-claim to be democratic republics, but the system designs vary hugely regarding limiting the power of state leaders and representative institutions, as well as the degree of checks and balances. Representative democratic countries' granularity resiliency index is roughly distributed between 0.14 and 0.22. Their granularity democracy index is about 0.15.

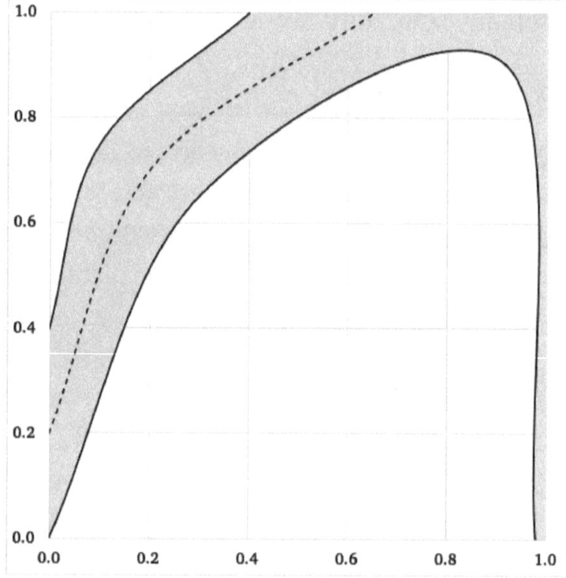

Figure 9.6 Granularity map: Representative democracy

While comparing the granularity maps of autocracy and representative democracy, a distinction stands out: The granularity pattern of autocracy, but not representative democracy, covers the upper left corner of the chart. This indicates that the public opinion boundary of representative democracy prevents high-rank decision-makers from interfering with the decisions on micro public affairs. This reveals an important revelation: When the head of state and top leaders cannot directly interfere with the life of individual citizens and community affairs, middle-level decision-makers do not have to succumb to the pressure of the superior leaders to make some independent decisions, which will then significantly increase the public's sense of security and dignity, even if the decision-making system still has many other shortcomings. It is the real source of the superiority of representative democracies over autocracy. But at the same time, it is worth noticing that the representative democracy's granularity pattern falls into the upper half (authoritarian domain) for the most part, and even about a half falls into the top 20% area (dictatorial zone). From this perspective, representative democracy is indeed an autocracy with the highest happiness while being good at camouflage. However, in the granularity map, there is no real irresistible force that prevents the public opinion boundary from being pushed towards the upper left corner until it disappears; also, the institutional boundary is likely to continue to float towards the upper end. A series of specific subtle policy changes combined (such as expanding the authority of senior leaders, transferring decision-making power from the grass-roots level to the higher-level in the political structure, delegating the decision-making power of the representatives to the administrative bureaucracy, and the prolonged absence of any meaningful referendum, etc.) can quietly transform a representative democracy nation into a de facto autocratic regime.

Slavery Democracy may be a somewhat contradictory name, but two seemingly opposing political systems are often combined to operate under the same framework. Their typical feature is that society is divided into two major classes: the ruling class and the governed mass. The ruling class may adopt some degree of democracy for policymaking, while the governed mass has no say in public affairs decisions at all. The ancient Greek republic was a classic slavery democracy[1], but such institutions could also emerge in other forms. For example, under the aristocratic or caste system, the ruling class of the noble or high caste may adopt some democratic way to make decisions, while the governed mass has no say. Early America is another example[2]; while the white people of the ruling class practiced representative democracy, people of color were either slaves or semi-slaves.

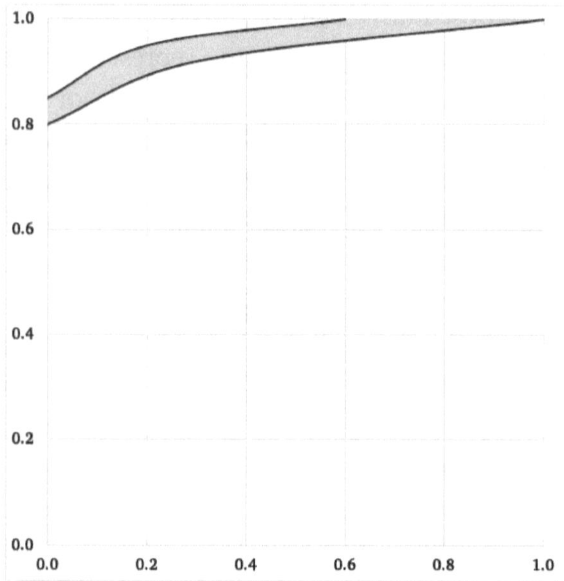

Figure 9.7 Granularity map: Slavery democracy

Certain modern oligopolistic or elitist countries also fall into this category. Within the ruling class composed of so-called social elites and privileged groups, some decisions are indeed made through democratic practices, but the general public outside the ruling class does not have any say over public affairs. Compared with other earlier slavery democracies, such countries do not always divide ruling or governed classes by natural identities, but instead often classify them by other conditions, such as family background, political stance, financial state, social status, etc. As such, some people in the lower class can enter the ruling class through marriage, political trust, trading of power and money, or gaining academic achievements. These channels give a certain degree of mobility between the two classes. To whitewash this inelegant reality, these regimes often designed so-called democratic activities which have neither substance nor influence over important policies. Nevertheless, the granularity map clearly reveals the nature of its dual society and the truth that elite groups carry out so-called "paternalistic" slavery against the majority.

As shown in Figure 9.7, the shape of slavery democracy's granular pattern is quite similar to that of representative democracy, except its position in the map has been compressed to the dictatorial zone at the top. It illustrates its unique nature: a combination of representative democracy enjoyed by the minority and absolute tyranny by the majority. The granularity resiliency index of this pattern is about 0.05. Its granularity democracy index is 0 (the elites in the ruling class may be reluctant about this, but in terms of the whole society, this value is entirely accurate).

For **_Micro-democracy_**, decision-making power's distribution is absolute, while its concentration is relative. Regardless of whether or not they set some voting delegation, citizens can always cast the direct vote and skip all delegation rules, which means the people hold complete control over all public affairs decisions. Although this is an exceptional situation from the perspective of overall statistics, from individual citizens' viewpoint, the act and power of direct voting is by no means an extreme situation, but an elemental right and norm. Realistically, citizens are more likely to choose to delegate to make the most of the non-critical daily decisions. Therefore, the granularity pattern covers the whole bottom of the granularity map, and advances towards the top; the higher it goes the larger the proportion citizens choose to delegate, or the higher the concentration of subjects. In the area to the left of the lower object granularity values, the granularity pattern has an upward limit and cannot reach the top. This is because, according to the micro-democracy principle of relevance, only local residents can decide on regional matters, and other citizens have no right to interfere. Therefore, even if all citizens who are entitled to decide on regional matters delegate the vote to a particular leader, it is still only partially representative of the whole people. The curve of the upper edge of the granularity pattern is called the *Micro-democracy Boundary*. Clearly, with the increase of the object granularity, this boundary progresses higher until it ends at the upper right corner of the chart. It reflects the extreme situation that all citizens autonomously delegate to one leader for national affairs. Of course, this is only a theoretical scenario. From a practical perspective, the possibility that all citizens in the country will delegate the voting to the same leader is almost non-existent.

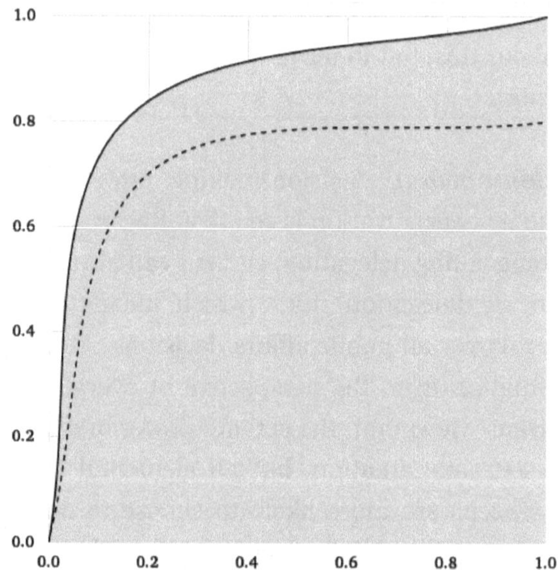

Figure 9.8 Granularity map: Micro-democracy

As shown in Figure 9.8, the granularity map, micro-democracy granularity resiliency index can reach above 0.85, while its granularity democratic index can reach 1.0.

From the above analysis, the upper and lower edges of the micro-democracy granularity pattern are extreme conditions. In most everyday situations, a micro-democracy society will operate in the middle range, rarely reaching the dictatorial zone near the upper edge. Additionally, some mandatory institutional rules can help to ensure sufficient dispersion among decision-makers, preventing the granularity pattern from falling into the dictatorial zone. For example, micro-democracy can mandate the minimum proportion and number of individual citizens for being public opinion agents; in such cases, it is statistically impossible that all the delegations will point to the same person, regardless of whether he or she is an independent citizen or a leader of political organizations. As reflected in the granularity map, the above institutional measures further push the micro-democracy boundary down until it falls outside the dictatorial zone, as the dashed line shows in Figure 9.8.

In the granularity maps, the granularity patterns of autocracy and micro-democracy are almost entirely reversed. Micro-democracy decision-making principles make it impossible to be incorporated into, or ever transformed into, an autocracy system through revising and tampering. Furthermore, between the granularity maps of representative democracy and micro-democracy, their granularity patterns only overlap in the range of grass-roots decision-making. This means that micro-democracy has brought many more civil rights and social choices to the public.

The above granularity analysis reveals the decision-making patterns, system resiliency, and degrees of democracy for different political systems. It helps more accurately identify the types and characteristics of political decision-making in specific countries and regimes, concluding with objective qualitative classification. After all, nothing is more misleading and deceptive than hiding the true nature of a political system in the title of a country and the names of institutions.

However, the decision-making pattern is not the only factor that measures the level of democracy. No matter how democratic the decision-making method is, if the decision is made based on misinformation and disinformation, then its outcome will only benefit the information manipulator rather than contributing to social utility. Such a country is just a democratic zombie. George Washington once said: *"An uninformed populace is a populace in slavery."* This claim has special warning significance for citizens of those self-claimed democratic regimes. When citizens of "democratic countries" are blocked from the truth by so-called "state secrets," when they treat the "mainstream media" as an authoritative source of information, when they are forced to tolerate the "goodwill protection" of content auditors and the "personalized feeding" of artificial intelligence on social media, then these people are indeed an "uninformed populace." Those cleverly packaged misleading messages are actually the "invisible hands" that turn citizens into voting puppets to make "sincere" decisions against their own interests. In a sense, these people are even more pathetic than plain slaves who can at least throw indifference and angry eyes at slave owners, while the democratic society slaves are often defenders of their own cage with a sense of advantage.

Therefore, *Public Decision-making Information Index (PDII)* is introduced here as another necessary factor in assessing the degree of social democracy. It measures how accurate and complete the information, which public decision-making relies on, is.

> **Public Decision-making Information Index =**
> Public Affair Decision-making Information Accessibility Index ×
> Information Credibility Index
>
> **PDII** = PADIAI•ICI
> Or, **PDII** = p4i•ICI

Public Affair Decision-making Information Accessibility Index (*PADIAI* or abbreviated as *p4i*) mentioned in the formula refers to the completeness of the information public can access for public affair decisions. Among them, *Public Affair Decision-making Information* (*PADI*) refers to information potentially influential and valuable for public affairs decisions. In the context of a country, all information should be public affairs decision-making information, except for citizens' private information and private companies' trade secrets. *Information Credibility Index* (*ICI*) in the formula refers to how authentic the information being accepted by the public in decision-making, is.

The above formula seems straightforward and intuitive but is hard to quantify. The ways of quantifying all public affairs decision-making information in a country, quantifying the parts directly or indirectly accessible to the public, and measuring the credibility of all this information, will be full of controversy. To make it convenient and practical, it is necessary to simplify it approximately while keeping the numerical qualitative range roughly accurate.

Among them, the *Public Affair Decision-making Information Accessibility Index* can be approximately defined with the following formula:

Public Affair Decision-making Information Accessibility Index = Proportion of Public Affairs Decision-making Information that citizens can obtain anonymously × The extent to which the above information can be used in a timely manner

It is useful to decompose *Public Affairs Decision-making Information* into two primary sources: governmental and social, and then further decompose the first parameter into two channels: active release and passive disclosure. In addition, the timely use of information is mainly attributed to its dissemination efficiency. The formula can be further simplified to:

Public Affair Decision-making Information Accessibility Index =
(Government Processed Information Effective Publish Ratio × W_1 +
Government Raw Information Effective Access Ratio × W_2 + Social
Information Effective Publish Ratio × W_3) ×
Public Information Dissemination Efficiency Index

PADIAI = (GPIEPR•W_1 + GRIEAR•W_2 + SIEPR•W_3) •PIDEI
Or, **p4i** = (gp•W_1 + gr•W_2 + si•W_3) •de

In the above formula, *Government Processed Information Effective Publish Ratio* (*GPIEPR*, or *gp* for short) refers to the degree to which the government actively publishes information. *Government Raw Information Effective Access Ratio* (*GRIEAR*, or *gr* for short) refers to the extent to which the public can obtain the original data of internal government operations. *Social Information Effective Publish Ratio* (*SIEPR*, or *si* for short) refers to the extent of public accessibility for information released by ordinary citizens. The above three indexes have emphasized "effectiveness." On the one hand, it means that the information should be directly or indirectly accessible to the public anonymously; on the other hand, it refers to its timeliness, that is, the public should know the information in time to make informed decisions. The above three indices are also multiplied by their respective weighting factors W_1, W_2, and W_3 for optimizing the accuracy of the formula. *Public Information Dissemination Efficiency Index* (*PIDEI*, or *de* for short) refers to the efficiency with which information is distributed across the public domain, especially the extent to which the public obtains time-sensitive published information before making decisions.

Again, these indexes are not quantified; their metrics are still complex and controversial. Among them, the measurement of government information is particularly challenging. The government's internal data and information processing usually are not transparent to the outside world. Due to the complexity of government bureaucracy and the existence of shadow governments, how much information is classified as confidential is not only unknown to the public but mysterious even to government officials. Some sensitive information may never be officially recorded and may be destroyed or hidden. Therefore, the total amount of government information is difficult to quantify, and the proportion of information that is publicly available is hence impossible to calculate. In this case, the quantification can still only be simplified by approximation. It should be noted that this is not the only or optimal approximate quantization scheme; it is entirely possible to be replaced by other more reasonable options.

In this approximate quantification scheme, all regular employees of the government are grouped by department and assigned a corresponding calculated share according to the headcounts. For example, if a government has 20 departments, and the Commerce Department hires 3% of the total government employees, then the overall share of the Commerce Department in the calculation of the information index is correspondingly 3%. Obviously, all 20 departments' percentages will sum up to 100%.

When calculating *Government Processed Information Effective Publish Ratio*, the total information share of all departments that meet the effective release criteria is the *gp* of the government as a whole. For example, if the effective release criteria are defined as 1) the department releases complete critical data, 2) incident reports to the society at a frequency not less than once every two weeks, and 3) the published data can be instantly and anonymously obtained by the public, then the sum of the calculated shares of all government departments that meet the criteria is the *gp* of that government at that time. For example, if only the Agriculture Department, the Commerce Department, and the Education Department reached the standard, and their employees accounted for 2.5%, 3.0%, and 17.2% of all government headcounts respectively, the government *gp* at this time was 22.7%.

Similarly, the determination criteria for *gr* can be defined as 1) all internal data and documents of the department are entirely open to the public, and 2) the public can access them in full digitally and instantly or view the paper copies that are two weeks older. Then the sum of the shares of all government departments that meet the criteria is the *gr* of that government at that time. Obviously, the government information involved in *gr* is a superset of that of *gp*. The reason why this overlap is allowed in this quantification scheme is that although *gr* better serves the integrity and accuracy, its qualification criteria exceed the realistic level that any current government can achieve. In the case where the *gr* index is almost always 0, the introduction of a lower standard *gp* helps to distinguish the level of information disclosure for current governments. By adjusting the ratio of W_1 and W_2, in the future, when micro-democracy and other forms of government have a non-0 *gr*, its weight can be made higher to approach the original intention of the *p4i* calculation.

In this approximative quantification scheme, *Social Information Effective Publish Ratio* is defined such that 1) the public can freely publish information to social media platforms, 2) information can be freely and anonymously accessed by the people on the platform, and 3) information will be retained for a long enough time so that it may be fully retrieved and disseminated. Judging by this definition, the adequate disclosure of social information may only occur in the era of network and popularization. Before this, it's not technically feasible. Its calculation formula can be embodied as:

Social Information Effective Publish Ratio =
Information Free Publisher Citizen Ratio ×
Information Free Receiver Citizen Ratio ×
Information Reliable Survival Ratio

SIEPR = IFPCR•IFRCR•IRSR
Or, **si** = ipr•irr•isr

Among them, *Information Free Publisher Citizen Ratio* (*IFPCR*, or *ipr* for short) refers to the proportion of the total population that can freely publish information to public information platforms. *Information Free Citizens Citizen Ratio Receiver Citizen Ratio* (*IFRCR*, or *irr* for short) refers to the proportion of the total population that can anonymously obtain information from public information platforms. The former is not limited to anonymous or real name publishing, because real name publishing helps the assessment of information's credibility, while the latter emphasizes anonymity because it eases the information access. *Information Reliable Survival Ratio* (*IRSR*, or *isr* for short) refers to the proportion of information that is accessible and that survives long enough (such as 30 days) on the public information platform without been tampered with, shielded, and deleted. This statistical data may not be actively provided by public information platforms, especially when the information is severely blocked or tampered with, but some technologies, like web crawlers or network sniffing, can observe the data from outside and learn about it indirectly. Further, the value of *Social Information Effective Publish Ratio* is dynamic. Most of the time, the government may not or only slightly interfere with the release of information. But during emergencies, it may interfere heavily or even block it completely. So, the minimum value measured over a long period more accurately reveals the degree to which a regime controls social information.

Public information dissemination methods roughly fall into two categories: centralized and distributed. The former is to broadcast information to the public through a central publishing channel, like news media and official government announcements. The latter is information spread by the public through free forwarding. Each has its pros and cons: The centralized method has extremely high delivery efficiency and can pass information to the entire society in almost real-time, but the content is extremely limited, and the publishing channel is subject to selective filtering, misleading interpretation, and so on; delivery speed for the distributed method is relatively slow, but the content has the broadest coverage. The downside is, it is subject to be tampered and forged during the forwarding, so information quality is even lower. Therefore, the efficiency of public information dissemination should be measured differently for these two dissemination methods.

In this approximate quantification scheme, *Public Information Dissemination Efficiency Index* is defined by the following formula:

Public Information Dissemination Efficiency Index =
(Centralized Transfer Channel Public Coverage ×
Centralized Transfer Channel Dispersion Ratio × deW_1)
+
(Distributed Transfer Channel Public Coverage ×
Distributed Transfer Channel Information Traceability × deW_2)

PIDEI = CTCPC•CTCDR•deW_1 + DTCPC•DTCIT•deW_2
Or, **de** = c3c•c3r•deW_1 + d3c•d3t•deW_2

In the above formula, *Centralized Transfer Channel (CTC)* is defined as any channel that can actually push information directly to more than 1% of the population. The emphasis is on actual delivery rather than the ability to deliver. For example, a television station's signal coverage can be 10% of the total population. However, unless its actual audience reaches 1% of the population, it is not counted. *Centralized Transfer Channel Public Coverage (CTCPC, or c3c for short)* refers to the proportion of the public covered by all centralized transfer channels that meet the above criteria. Its value ranges from 0 to 1. A larger value indicates that more people are covered. *Distributed Transfer Channel Public Coverage (DTCPC, or d3c for short)* refers to the proportion of the total population that can freely access the information platform. Its value ranges from 0 to 1. A larger value indicates more people can access the platform.

Centralized Transfer Channel Dispersion Ratio (*CTCDR*, or *c3r* for short) is calculated with the following formula:

Centralized Transfer Channel Dispersion Ratio =
Number of Centralized Transfer Channel Independent Controllers ÷
Number of Centralized Transfer Channels

$$\textbf{CTCDR} = \frac{NCTCIC}{NCTC} \quad \text{Or, } \textbf{c3r} = \frac{n4c}{n2c}$$

Among them, *Centralized Transmission Channel Independent Controllers* (*NCTCIC*, or *n4c* for short) refers to those entities that control the daily operation and content of centralized transfer channels through financial holding or administrative jurisdiction. For example, the same consortium controls multiple news organizations, or, in this case, the same government runs various state-owned news organizations. *Number of Centralized Transfer Channels* (*NCTC*, or *n2c* for short) refers to the total number of these channels. According to this formula, the value of *Centralized Transfer Channel Dispersion Ratio* ranges from 0 to 1. A larger value indicates a higher degree of dispersion.

Distributed Transmission Channel Information Traceability (*DTCIT*, or *d3t* for short) refers to the proportion of information that can be traced back to the original publisher in the distributed transfer channels. This traceability directly relates to the information platform's ability to detect and correct information tampering and forgery, and there are many technical means capable of achieving this.

In addition, deW_1 and deW_2 in the above formulas are weight adjustment factors of the centralized and distributed methods, used to optimize the formula.

Active and free information exchange and dissemination should have significantly improved the quality of public decision-making. However, if this information is mixed with a lot of misinformation and disinformation, making it impossible for the public to distinguish the truth, then the benefits of more information are completely offset, and sometimes even more dangerous than no information. Modern technology can make the forgery of information more real and can spread rumors faster. Once the information dissemination channels are maliciously manipulated, higher *Public Affair Decision-making Information Accessibility Index* (*PADIAI*) may also mean worse disruption. Therefore, it is necessary to introduce the *Information Credibility Index* (*ICI*) in the formula of *Public Decision-making Information Index* (*PDII*) to adjust the possible bias.

Understanding things is usually a progression of development and improvement, and the truth often reveals itself through a process of first understanding something partially and working towards full comprehension. Throughout the process, many facts and truths that people once believed sincerely are often later found to be incomplete or even wrong. Such kind of "sincere mistakes" have happened throughout history and naturally have caused various controversies. If people can understand and accept the reasonable defects in the process of learning with tolerance and rationality, they will approach the truth in a much smoother manner. Therefore, the introduction of *Information Credibility Index* is not for judging right or wrong but identifying malicious tampering and fabrication.

The *Information Credibility Index* still needs some approximate quantification scheme. The scheme proposed here is based on the following two assumptions: First, if an individual or organization associates the credibility of information with their public credit and reputation, the information usually is more trustworthy. On the flip side, when more information can be clearly associated with reputation endorsement, people can more accurately assess the credibility of the information, so they can select information with better quality for making decisions. The formula for this approximate quantization scheme is:

Information Credibility Index =
Average Time of Consumption of Traceable Information ÷
Average Total Time of Consumption of All Information

$$\mathbf{ICI} = \frac{ATCTI}{ATTCAI} \quad \text{Or,} \quad \mathbf{ICI} = \frac{a3i}{a4i}$$

In the above formula, *Average Time of Consumption of Traceable Information* (*ATCTI*, or *a3i* for short) refers to the average time spent by the public on viewing traceable information, and *Average Total Time of Consumption of All Information* (*ATTCAI*, or *a4i* for short) refers to the average time spent by the public on all information. Among them, *Traceable Information* refers to any information that can be reliably, directly or indirectly, traced back to the original publisher. Typically, it includes books with identifiable authors, files associated with traceable collectors and recorders, audio, and video with real name producers, etc. Any anonymously provided information does not qualify. The reliability of traceability is a crucial factor but easy to be left out, so it deserves special attention. Generally speaking, information coming directly from the original publisher is considered reliably traceable. Forwarded information, even if marked by the original publishers, is normally regarded as unreliable. This is because the publisher data and information content may have been tampered with during the retransmission unless the message carries a link directly pointing to the original publishing source or complete records of forwarding chain (including all the forwarders' data, supplemented with technical means to verify the data's authenticity). According to this formula, the value range of the *Information Credibility Index* is from 0 to 1. The larger the value, the more credible the information is. Obviously, retrieving the above data requires some sampling and statistics, but it is relatively easy to collect.

At this point, the modeling of *Public Decision-making Information Index* (*PDII*) is complete. Its combination with *Political Decision Granularity Analysis* (*PDGA*) produces a mathematic way to research the mode of decision-making and degree of democracy for given governments and society. In the following formula, *National Democracy Index* (*NDI*) reveals the degree of democracy of a given regime. The larger the value, the higher the degree of democracy.

National Democracy Index =
Political Decision-making Granularity Democracy Index ×
Public Decision-making Information Index

$$\textbf{NDI} = PDGDI \cdot PDII$$

This index will help people directly and objectively measure the degree of democracy of various countries, without being confused and distracted by names of the nation, forms of the governments, structures of power institutions, processes of the power exercise, and the legal systems. Besides, the distribution and operation of state power are not always stable; they are often in adjustment with the game between internal forces and changes in external conditions. Therefore, in the overall study of the political state of a country, slice sampling for different years and periods, trending analysis, is always desired.

From the above analysis, we can clearly see that *National Democracy Index* of a micro-democracy society is higher than of any other political system that has ever existed, and its democratic advancement and authenticity can be recognized and proven scientifically. Further, with the help of information technology, the *National Democracy Index* of a micro-democracy country will likely approach its highest limit. If this becomes a reality, then a micro-democracy society will reach the highest state of democracy in human civilization.

Conclusion

Born after the World Wars, most of us have not experienced the darkest moments and deepest suffering of human civilization. The prosperity of the market economy and the leap of technology have brought us superior living conditions and unprecedented optimism. The times we live in should be the best that humans have ever experienced.

However, the dark force in people's hearts is still lurking, waiting for the call of the eye of Sauron. The shell of the old world has sheltered this force. If human civilization cannot transcend itself, then the darkness will make a comeback. During the time this book was written, the world has also undergone rapid changes. Human civilization seems to be sliding towards some deep crisis, and gloomy dark clouds are rolling in from the horizon. The once positive, optimistic, developmental, and harmonious atmosphere has been swallowed by the uneasy feelings of fragmentation, conflict, and mistrust, and dangerous confrontations or even wars seem to be imminent. Human society has lost its way and is wandering, mired in confusion and anxiety. However, this is not due to the deterioration of people's consciousness, but rather their awakening. After the democratic camp and the capitalist camp won the Cold War, they gradually lost the cover and camouflage of their shortcomings. Surrounded by borderless capitals, the so-called New World Order swept the battlefield of victory, revealing its profit-seeking and bloodthirsty nature. For trading of power and interests, those transnational elites never mind paying the cost of people's living conditions and even lives. When people dimly see the truth, they become disillusioned with the fairytale of globalization; then isolationism, nationalism, nationalism and the law of the jungle are revived. Although primitive and cruel, they are at least complying with common sense and are real. Regrettably, the old world's order did not come to save the masses. It was just the wealthy lords collecting their lost treasures.

The key to finding the antidote is power. People need to learn to see naked power through dazzling flames and smoke. As long as there is a concentration of power in the political structure, it will never be possible to truly achieve social justice and equality. The spots where power gather will always be the target of erosion and the fulcrum of manipulation by special interest groups, and democratic regimes are no exception. The more unfair social distribution becomes, the more unequal people's power, the more stressful the lives of ordinary people, and the easier the ruling class to manipulate and enslave the masses. Therefore, power is willing to allow, encourage, and even deliberately create such stratifications and divisions among peoples. The development of science and information technology cannot automatically change this tendency. In fact, with the rapid increase in social wealth and material supplies, ordinary people are more anxious, and the workload and working hours have increased instead of dropping. The value-oriented commodity society is desperately creating new demands for people, and to answer these emerging new demands, people have to work harder under higher pressure. The root cause of all these is that the consumption and distribution of human and material resources in today's society is driven by money and capital, which is dominated by a tiny number of elites, rather than by the general public's wishes. This driving mechanism relies on collusions and money-power transactions by financial oligarchs and political elites to be effective. Once the power of the political elite is crippled or even removed as designed in the micro-democracy system, the financial oligarchs and the capitalist class must directly face the requests of all citizens and lose the lever of manipulation. It is only then when their power will naturally and significantly weaken. In that case, we can even infer with optimism that they will adapt and evolve until they are tamed as allies of the public, and gradually become contributors to the overall happiness and utility of society.

If those above mentioned socio-political and economic evolutions have some historical inevitability and will occur naturally sooner or later, then we may not have to rush to act. Rather, we can wait with patience for micro-democracy or other superior social forms to evolve and mature. However, while writing this book, I constantly saw the rulers and vested interests of the old world fighting back fiercely, trying to use the power of technology and information to create potent tools of domination. When they have absolute control over technology and information, they will gain overwhelming power that all human beings cannot compete with and make their ruling and slavery even crueler. With advanced technology, open and hidden dictators can fool, control, and enslave the public with ease, even without a big army. It is the real leading threat and decisive weapon in human history. Every minute, the old forces are trying to start a new war, fueling their killing machine with the blood and flesh of millions of people. Every minute, they are also accelerating the depletion of the earth's natural resources, polluting and destroying the ecosystem, exchanging the entire future of humanity for immediate profits. Therefore, depriving the power of the old forces, and dissolving them forever is not only necessary but also surpassing urgency. It is a race and battle between the people and rulers of the world.

As Ronald Reagan once said, *"Freedom is never more than one generation away from extinction. We didn't pass it to our children in the bloodstream. It must be fought for, protected, and handed on for them to do the same."*[1] This battle cannot be waited for or delayed. As men and women of this era, this is our revolution, and this is our responsibility. May we work together so that people will eventually live freely, lovingly, and happily!

Postscript

After I started this book on a winter night in St. Petersburg a few years ago, the slow progress of writing has often caught me in anxiety. What allows me to comfort myself is that although I have seen some apparent social bearings and the urgency of change, the world is still showing dance and wine, and it seems that the storm is still far away, so I can feel relief with my procrastination. Since I completed writing a few months ago and started to translate it into English, the atmosphere of the world has changed disturbingly, and the situation has rapidly deteriorated in an unimaginable manner. At the moment when I finally finished all the work today, the world is in a deep crisis with the plague spreading, the economy collapsing, public resentment escalating, and the hostility between countries sharply rising. It seems that humanity is slipping into an abyss of conflict and suffering. This is the very moment people badly need new ideas and solutions to get rid of this disaster and move towards a bright and hopeful future. This may be the destiny that God has arranged for this book.

This unexpected plague offers a case study for micro-democracy to imagine different possibilities through making some assumptions.

Regarding the origin of the virus, there have been various claims made all over, including many conspiracy theories. I will not comment on this for the time being, nor intend to sell my speculation to my readers. Although the truth is covered, it always exists somewhere, lying quietly in a corner or hiding in someone's heart. The reason for the cover-up is mostly because the old politicians are either to evade accountability for their faults, or to maintain their power and rulings, or to take advantage of opportunities to attack rivals, or deliberately confuse the audiovisual for other purposes. In the final analysis, it is to deceive the public and use the people to serve their selfish interests. In a micro-democracy world, a world without old politicians and rulers, with complete transparency of information, this accident may not even happen in the first place. Even if it does happen, people can learn the truth and make the most effective response instead of wasting time and energy in the wrong direction or becoming suspicious of each other and making accusations, which could even lead to possible conflicts and wars.

If the origin of the virus is still controversial, the loss of control at the beginning of the outbreak is a human disaster without question. In the first few weeks, information suppression for political reasons made people lose the best chance to stop the spread of the virus. When the infection spread all over the world, deliberate neglect and understatement for political reasons, combined with the inability of the political system, made people lose the best timing for medical and financial preparation. The loss of these opportunities has unnecessarily cost lives and economic losses by thousands of folds. Again, in a micro-democracy world where there are no old politicians and rulers, and the information is completely transparent, this is also avoidable. In particular, the knowledge-based voting weights of micro-democracy decision-making can make a huge difference. By leveraging the sum of medical and economic knowledge of the whole society, people will make more informed, balanced, and rapid responses based on fully understanding the real-time situation, instead of falling into passive guessing and waiting.

In the course of responding to the pandemic, the vulnerabilities of some developed market economy countries have been fully exposed. In some of the richest countries in the world, due to long-term polarization, the rich have everything, but the poor struggle on the edge of survival. Once a disaster occurs, the survival line of the poor collapses immediately. They lose their livelihood, falling into trouble. In the micro-democracy world, personal life materials are the basic system of human rights, unconditionally guaranteed by the government. Basic lodging and food, medical care, and communications are essential supports for people's physical and mental health, allowing people to pass through difficult times with peace of mind.

The freedom of migration in micro-democracy institutional human rights may worry people whether such a flow of migrants will cause the pandemic to spread. In fact, micro-democracy has designed some emergency procedures for special periods such as war, plague, and natural disasters, allowing people to take reasonable measures, including setting temporary restrictions on institutional human rights to respond to crises effectively. The design of the processes can be found in the chapters *Human Rights* and *Government*. In particular, it is necessary to point out that rulers of certain countries have exploited this opportunity of the epidemic to actively expand their power, especially by further restricting control of information. People should be alarmed and pay special attention to this regression in democracy and the restoration of autocracy. In the design of micro-democracy, it is particularly emphasized that temporary human rights restrictions for special periods require the authorization of the whole people, and there must be a reliable automated restoration mechanism.

The impact of the pandemic on the economy caused a huge secondary disaster. However, there are still some positive revelations that came out of it. First of all, the large-scale economic stagnation has not created a significant impact on people's living supplies, and the stocks of food and daily necessities are still abundant. This aspect shows that the level of social production is already very high, and the material reserves are also quite rich. On the other hand, it also demonstrates that most people's work is actually unnecessary. Agricultural production in the world already has large-scale mechanization capabilities, and only a small portion of people can produce enough food for all the people. Industrial production has also greatly exceeded the necessary level; it is only the deliberately created consumerist society that has created excessive demand. When people's lives were forced to stagnate, it was found that in truth, people's material needs can be much simpler, and the reduction in material needs also significantly lowered the labor demand of the manufacturing industry. In other words, only a small amount of industrial production and labor is needed to meet people's reasonable material needs. In fact, the reduction in industrial production has even produced some positive effects.[1] For example, in less than two months, the world's total greenhouse gas emissions have fallen by 5%, and the consumption of natural resources has also dropped dramatically. People have proven that a healthy economic model can effectively reverse the trend of climate warming and ecological deterioration.

Therefore, the impact of the pandemic on people's lives is definitely not caused by the shortage of materials, but ultimately the failure of the material distribution, or the failure of the market economic system that determines the material distribution mechanism. The reason is very simple: We have learned that the world's food and materials are adequately supplied and only require a small amount of labor. But still, most people's food and living materials must be satisfied (otherwise it will cause social unrest and political collapse), such that the essence of the problem becomes how to distribute food and materials to most people who do not produce them. The market economy's solution is to create and expand the tertiary industry—namely the service sector. The food that people can eat is limited, and the clothing they wear is limited, but the services they can enjoy are unlimited. Moreover, in this process, capitalists can also exploit surplus value. This strategy has indeed kept the problem at bay for a long time. Unfortunately, this mechanism has developed to the extreme, and people have to work too much unnecessarily, and are unable to fully enjoy the benefits that human civilization has to offer. However, the pandemic completely crashed the service sector[2], which put the market economy in a desperate situation.

Faced with economic desperation, the instinctive reaction of capitalist society is normally war. On the one hand, it sets up enemies to shirk the responsibility of politicians' dereliction of duty and covers up the structural defects of the market economy. On the other hand, it creates material and labor demand through war. In essence, it saves the market economy system with a cost of tremendous lives and material loss. Of course, there is always a possibility that all humanity will face difficulties together and overcome the challenges together. But this requires a strong force of peace and the power of love for life. For this vision, the modern countries are precisely its natural enemy, and the old politicians who live under the shell of the modern state act like the virus. There is a phenomenon, in the fight against the virus, wherein the internals of various countries will work together relatively, but between countries, they fight with each other, blame each other, and even obstruct the flow of medical supplies and food to the places with most urgent needs. All these acts exacerbated the humanitarian crisis. Viruses see no borders, but national borders create another kind of disease, which impedes the blood flow of human society and worsens the symptoms.

Apparently, micro-democracy can solve these problems entirely by eliminating modern nations. However, in fact, without having to adopt such a seemingly radical approach, the design of the micro-democracy education system alone is sufficient to provide a third road to solve the current economic dilemma. That is to say, replacing the service sector with the education sector in the market economy. The education sector will become the emerging fourth industry so that the distribution of materials can be carried out in a way compatible with the market economy. Since the job supply of the education sector is infinite, and its demand for material support is deficient, it will be completely unaffected by disasters so that the regular and orderly social operation is maintained. It will not only resolve the short-term crisis of the market economy, but it may also become an opportunity for a country to surpass other rivals and achieve a leap in technology. Since the social supply of food and materials is inevitable, why not transform it into an investment and driving force for social progress? Why not maximize its effect?

At this moment, the world is still in the most profound crisis. People are still in a state of panic, fear, sadness, anger, and hatred. However, the disaster will eventually pass like a dream, and people will start living again. But life will no longer be the same as it once was. People have seen the various perils lurking in this system, this society, and this world, and they will undoubtedly make different choices for the future. I hope this book will show people a new path, a path to the light.

Let me end this book with John Lennon's famous quote[3]:

Imagine there's no countries, it isn't hard to do
Nothing to kill or die for, and no religion too
Imagine all the people living life in peace

Imagine no possessions, I wonder if you can
No need for greed or hunger, a brotherhood of man
Imagine all the people sharing all the world

You may say I'm a dreamer, but I'm not the only one
I hope someday you'll join us, and the world will be as one

Aaron Ran

aaron.ran@microdemocracy.com
http://www.microdemocracy.com
Tennessee, USA, April 5th, 2020

Notes

Preface

1. Bae, Hannah. "Bill Gates Emails Microsoft Employees to Celebrate Company's 40th Anniversary." *CNN Business*, CNN Money, Apr. 2015, money.cnn.com/2015/04/05/technology/bill-gates-email-microsoft-40-anniversary/index.html.
2. Hegel, Georg Wilhelm Friedrich, et al. *Elements of the Philosophy of Right.* Cambridge University Press, 1991.
3. Driver, Julia. "The History of Utilitarianism." *Stanford Encyclopedia of Philosophy*, Stanford University, 22 Sept. 2014, plato.stanford.edu/entries/utilitarianism-history/.

Chapter 1 Vote

1. *Universal Declaration of Human Rights.* United Nations, 1948.
2. The Editors of Encyclopedia Britannica. "Ecclesia." *Encyclopedia Britannica*, Encyclopedia Britannica, Inc., 2 Apr. 2018, www.britannica.com/topic/Ecclesia-ancient-Greek-assembly.
3. Speck, Bruno Wilhelm, and Wagner Pralon Mancuso. "A Study on the Impact of Campaign Finance, Political Capital and Gender on Electoral Performance." *Brazilian Political Science Review*, vol. 8, no. 1, 2014, pp. 34–57., doi:10.1590/1981-38212014000100002.
4. Jhangiani, Dr. Rajiv, et al. "Biases in Attribution." *Principles of Social Psychology 1st International Edition*, BC Campus, 26 Sept. 2014, opentextbc.ca/socialpsychology/chapter/biases-in-attribution/.
5. Smaldone, David. "The Role of Time in Place Attachment." *General Technical Report - Proceedings*, 2007, doi: https://www.fs.usda.gov/treesearch/pubs/12653.
6. Dennet, Daniel. "Theory of Mind." *The Oxford Handbook of Comparative Evolutionary Psychology*, by Jennifer Vonk and Todd K. Shackelford, Oxford University Press, 2012, pp. 53–54.

Chapter 3 Procedure

1. Rousseau, Jean-Jacques, et al. *The Social Contract.* Penguin, 2004.

Chapter 4 Human Rights

1. Triandis, Harry C. *Individualism and Collectivism.* Routledge, 2019.
2. Berrill, Kenneth, and T. S. Ashton. "The Industrial Revolution 1760-1830." *The Economic Journal*, vol. 59, no. 235, 1949, p. 403., doi:10.2307/2226873.
3. *Universal Declaration of Human Rights.* United Nations, 1948

4. Maslow, Abraham H. "A Theory of Human Motivation." *Psychological Review*, vol. 50, no. 4, 1943, pp. 370396., doi:10.1037/h0054346.

5. "FAO Cereal Supply and Demand Brief." *World Food Situation*, Food and Agriculture Organization of the United Nations, www.fao.org/worldfoodsituation/csdb/en/.

6. Smith, Adam. *The Wealth of Nations*. W. Strahan and T. Cadell, London, 1776.

7. Wood, John Cunningham. *Karl Marx's Economics: Critical Assessments*. Routledge, 1991.

8. United Nations. "YouthStats: Education." *United Nations Youth Envoy*, Office of the Secretary-General's Envoy on Youth, 2015, www.un.org/youthenvoy/youth-statistics-education/.

Chapter 5 Law

1. Rheinstein, Max, and Mary Ann Glendon. "Civil Law." *Encyclopedia Britannica*, Encyclopedia Britannica, Inc., 16 Oct. 2019, www.britannica.com/topic/civil-law-Romano-Germanic.

2. Healy, Nicholas Joseph. "Maritime Law." *Encyclopedia Britannica*, Encyclopedia Britannica, Inc., 22 Jan. 2020, www.britannica.com/topic/maritime-law.

Chapter 6 Government

1. The Editors of Encyclopedia Britannica. "Separation of Powers." *Encyclopedia Britannica*, Britannica, Inc., 10 Apr. 2020, www.britannica.com/topic/separation-of-powers.

Chapter 7 World

1. Chen, James. "Return on Investment (ROI)." *Investopedia*, Dotdash - Investopedia, 27 Apr. 2020, www.investopedia.com/terms/r/returnoninvestment.asp.

2. Twin, Alexandra. "Understanding Key Performance Indicators (KPIs)." *Investopedia*, Dotdash - Investopedia, 29 Jan. 2020, www.investopedia.com/terms/k/kpi.asp.

3. Hamann, Ralph, and Stephanie Bertels. "The Institutional Work of Exploitation: Employers' Work to Create and Perpetuate Inequality." *Journal of Management Studies*, vol. 55, no. 3, 2017, pp. 394–423., doi:10.1111/joms.12325.

Chapter 8 Road

1. Fukuyama, Francis. *The End of History and the Last Man*. Penguin, 1992.

2. Stalin, Joseph Vissarionovich. *Dialectical and Historical Materialism*. International Publishers, 1972.

3. Ziblatt, Daniel. "How Did Europe Democratize?" *World Politics*, vol. 58, no. 2, 2006, pp. 311–338., doi:10.1353/wp.2006.0028.

4. Skocpol, Theda. "Old Regime Legacies and Communist Revolutions in Russia and China." *Social Forces*, vol. 55, no. 2, 1976, p. 284., doi:10.2307/2576225.

5. Joosung, Rhie. "LABOUR INTENSITY AND SURPLUS VALUE IN KARL MARX - A NOTE." *History of Economic Ideas*, vol. 7, no. 3, 1999, pp. 181–191. *JSTOR*, www.jstor.org/stable/23722438. Accessed 1 July 2020.
6. Gören, Erkan. "How Ethnic Diversity Affects Economic Growth." *World Development*, vol. 59, 2014, pp. 275–297., doi: 10.1016/j.worlddev.2014.01.012.
7. Alesina, Alberto, and Eliana La Ferrara. "Ethnic Diversity and Economic Performance." *NBER WORKING PAPER SERIES*, 2004, doi:10.3386/w10313.
8. Spark, Alasdair. "Conjuring Order: The New World Order and Conspiracy Theories of Globalization." *The Sociological Review*, vol. 48, no. 2_suppl, 2000, pp. 46–62., doi:10.1111/j.1467-954x.2000.tb03520. x.
9. "5 Things You Should Know About Mainframe Security." *PSR Incorporated*, 16 Jan. 2019, www.psrinfo.com/5-things-you-should-know-about-mainframe-security/.
10. Drolet, Michelle. "How a Decentralized Cloud Model May Increase Security, Privacy." *CSO Online*, CSO, 12 July 2019, www.csoonline.com/article/3405439/how-a-decentralized-cloud-model-may-increase-security-privacy.html.
11. Hulme, George V. "DDoS Explained: How Distributed Denial of Service Attacks Are Evolving." *CSO Online*, CSO, 13 Feb. 2020, www.csoonline.com/article/3222095/ddos-explained-how-denial-of-service-attacks-are-evolving.html.

Chapter 9 Science

1. Frank, Jill. "Athenian Democracy and Its Critics." *Ethnic and Racial Studies*, vol. 42, no. 8, 2019, pp. 1306–1312., doi:10.1080/01419870.2019.1586971.
2. Riley, Padraig. *Slavery and the Democratic Conscience: Political Life in Jeffersonian America*. University of Pennsylvania Press., 2016.

Conclusion

1. Reagan, Ronald. "Encroaching Control" Annual Meeting of the Phoenix Chamber of Commerce, 30 Mar 1961

Postscript

1. Quéré, Corinne Le, et al. "Temporary Reduction in Daily Global CO2 Emissions during the COVID-19 Forced Confinement." *Nature Climate Change*, vol. 10, no. 7, 2020, pp. 647–653., doi:10.1038/s41558-020-0797-x.
2. Guzman, Nicolas, et al. "Coronavirus' Impact on Service Organizations: Weathering the Storm." *McKinsey & Company*, 29 Apr. 2020, www.mckinsey.com/business-functions/operations/our-insights/coronavirus-impact-on-service-organizations-weathering-the-storm.
3. Lennon, John, et al. "John Lennon – Imagine." *Genius*, genius.com/John-lennon-imagine-lyrics.

www.ingramcontent.com/pod-product-compliance
Lightning Source LLC
Chambersburg PA
CBHW051443250726

48655CB00001B/211